"Tom Hohstadt's book offers a unique analysis of music composed for the modern screen. While traditional treatises have focused more on the aesthetics and mechanics of scoring to film, Dr. Hohstadt examines the psychology of screen music from the viewer's perspective. This book is a contemporary, thoughtful, and provocative presentation that will appeal to serious students of the film-music genre." **Daniel Allan Carlin, Emmy-winning Director of Scoring for Motion Pictures & Television; University of Southern California**

"*Film Music: a Journey of Felt Meaning* is not only a fascinating look into the world of film music but also a valuable introduction to the experiences possible through the cutting edge technology of virtual reality. This book is for anyone who appreciates suspending disbelief and the study of actual perception. Hohstadt's book illuminates the immense possibilities of virtual reality that may well lead us to reimagine our entire civilization." **Steven Argila, award-winning film and television composer, songwriter, and record producer**

"*Felt Meaning* makes a compelling case that film and film music are central in defining a new cannon of relevant literature for the 21st century. It's a wonderful teaching tool for both the musical and non-musical, and serves as a thoughtful, provocative exploration into the nature of media, artistic expression, and our relationships to it. If music is the ultimate metaphorical artistic language, Dr. Hohstadt's case for the position of film music at the center of our new ways of expressing timeless human values and aspirations feels spot on to me." **Jeff Beal, film composer, winner of 4 Emmy Awards**

"*Film Music* by Thomas Hohstadt is a highly intelligent deep dive into how film music is perceived today and how that perception has changed over time. Questions for the reader about personal reactions to suggested pieces of score add an interactive approach to this work. This book represents not just a treatise on the subject but an obvious culmination of years of inquisitive, intelligent thought." **Richard Bellis, author of *The Emerging Film Composer***

"As we enter a new age for virtual reality, it is most encouraging to find someone has looked at and listened to the art of the movie score and come up with a clear and creative way of understanding the sound behind the screen. Hohstadt examines the form with new eyes and ears, and gives us a roadmap to the future. He takes us by the hand, sits next to us in the darkened theatre and prods us, with gentle expertise, to open ourselves to the future." **Buz Kohan, Emmy winning writer, composer, and producer.**

"Bravo . . . I was very impressed with his breadth of ideas and concepts . . . very nicely presented with many fine examples of concepts to ponder . . . I would hope that all persons interested in film music would read this book . . . Great work!" **Dr. Larry M. Timm, author of** *The Soul of Cinema*

"Film Music: A Journey of Felt Meaning is an enlightening excursion inside the various difficult-to-define aspects of musical craft. Nestled somewhere between what is real, and what is imagined, author Tom Hohstadt attempts to push the understanding of how and why music works in film beyond that of mere words. Through deep emotional reflection, understanding of habits and history, and suggesting personal journeys, Hohstadt sparks the questions to the answers that only the listener can understand. He challenges the reader to not simply think of the meaning behind music, but rather feel it . . . very cool book, very different and thought-provoking." **Brian Satterwhite, award-winning film composer**

Film composers generally don't have time to consider how or why they are inspired to create their music. They are more concerned with the looming delivery deadline. But in this book Professor Hohstadt offers a well-reasoned analysis of the decisions composers make in response to the images with which they are presented. **Ashley Irwin, President, Society of Composers and Lyricists (working in Television and Motion Pictures)**

FILM MUSIC

A Journey of Felt Meaning

FILM MUSIC

A Journey of Felt Meaning

by

Thomas Hohstadt

Damah Media

2016

© 2016 Thomas Hohstadt

First Printing: 2016

ISBN 978-0-9672944-4-5

Publisher: Damah Media, 3522 Maple Avenue, Odessa, TX 79762; Phone 432-366-0457

Ordering Information:

Special discounts are available on quantity purchases by corporations, associations, educators, and others. For details, contact the publisher at the above listed address.

U.S. trade bookstores and wholesalers: Please contact Lulu.com at
http://www.lulu.com/contact-us

Dedication

To my students,

who convinced me we were on the right track.

Contents

Preface

My parents blessed me with the finest music education in America and Europe (the Eastman School of Music and the Akadamie für Musik in Vienna, Austria). I reveled in the best histories, theories, techniques, traditions and styles. I was ready to conquer the world.

So I thought.

In moments of honesty, I knew something was missing. And I often noticed similar emptiness at the performances of my favorite superstar conductors. It became a burning issue for me, and, as a result, my life became the search for what seemed to be the missing language of music.

This quest led to the study of metaphor, then the language of juxtaposition, and finally to virtual reality. My concerts became laboratory experiments of virtual reality—not as a technology, but as a language and an art form.

In 2012, the University of Texas of the Permian Basin asked me to write an online course on the subject. Student response was enthusiastic and they soon demanded "Virtual Reality II"!

Film Music is the result and the reader will recognize many of the ideas from my earlier book: *The Age of Virtual Reality*.

I. INTRODUCTION

An Alternative World

It no longer makes sense to say, "Let's go to the movies." We're already there! The many screens in our make-believe world are increasingly becoming the world in which we live. For some, it's still an "alternative world." Yet, for those who spend most of their waking lives in front of screens, it has become a "habitat." And for the rest of us, it is not far-fetched to suggest we are quickly migrating toward a full-fledged, in-your-face, surrogate reality.

Ready or not, the world of nonliteral images has become our refuge of fantasy. It has become our compelling mystery where imagined—and not so imagined—forces turn sensuous.

In this habitat of screens, we contemplate the unknown more than the known, the awe more than the ordinary, the mystery more than the mundane. We watch the instinct more than the intellect, the content more than the form, the message more than the medium. We feel the ecstasy more than the discipline, the compelling more than the control, the artistry more than the technique. In other words, life in front of screens marks a major shift from informed opinion to inspired intuition and from the literate to the visionary. "People are spending more time in media and especially screen media than anything else they're doing in life."[1] As a result, films and film music are becoming a less peripheral interest and a more intrinsic necessity.

This should be good news, for movies run exact parallels with past artistic achievements. The hidden feelings in both screen technology and the fine arts represent things not there, things unseen, things beyond themselves. Both screens and art represent things imagined that feel essentially real. Or, put another way, they both represent "serious make-believe."

Today's cinematic masterworks and their "screen" equivalents will surely become the highest art forms of this century.

"Inherently Bizarre?"

Not everyone agrees, though, for offended music historians still resist the claim.

"Movies weren't always considered art. How could a movie tell a story as well as a novel? And surely a movie is nothing but a poor imitation of a play—who would sit in front of a

---

[1] Bill Moult of Sequent Partners quoted in Higgins, Adrian, "We can't see the forest for the T-Mobiles" *Washington Post*, Tuesday, December 15, 2009; C01. (My italics and emphasis)

---

screen to watch a lousy recording when they could sit mere feet away from the actor himself, live and in the moment?"[2]

And the disreputable history of Hollywood hasn't helped. Oscar Levant famously admitted that its film industry had a lot of phony tinsel. But, he added, "Behind the phony tinsel of Hollywood lies the real tinsel."

Music, of course, was often a mere addition, distorted to fit the script. Any attempt by symphony conductors to present film music—by itself—on serious concerts was discouraging and awkward. First, the film owners often had no reason to make the music available, and, secondly, the music, itself, was inevitably a string of chopped audio clips with little internal relationship to themselves.[3]

Even today, the largest reference work on music in Western Civilization claims, "Musical

[2] Nicholas Deleon, "Are video games art?" *CrunchGear* http://tinyurl.com/y2k4bm3

[3] Thomas Hohstadt, "American Film Music: Art or Entertainment?" *The Cue Sheet* (The Newsletter of the Society for the Preservation of Film Music) Volume 5, No. 2, April 1988.

accompaniment to dramatic action is inherently bizarre in concept."[4]

Everything Has Changed

With these facts, the future of film and film music may not be so bright after all.

Yet, wait.

Something big is happening—even epic. The great thinkers are saying this "something" is slipping up on us suddenly, exponentially. Everything, including the future of the movie industry, is happening in an expanded *now*.

Ray Kurzweil, the great author, inventor, futurist, and director of engineering at Google, claims this moment in history will end 6,000 years of "civilization" as we have known it.[5] In the twenty-first century, according to Kurzweil, we'll see—at today's rate—on the order of

---

[4] Mervyn Cooke, "Film Music," Grove Music Online,
http://www.oxfordmusiconline.com.ezproxy.ut pb.edu/subscriber/article/grove/music/09647? qa=bizarre&search=search_in_article&button_ search.x=0&button_search.y=0#hit_in_article 1

[5] Ray Kurzweil, "Accelerated Living," *PC Magazine*, Vol. 20, No. 15, September 4, 2001, pp. 151-153.

20,000 years of change. Kurzweil claims technological progress in this century will be 1,000 times greater than in the last century. Time, in other words, has become "exponential." He explains it this way: "With 30 steps, you get to 30." "With 30 exponential steps, you get to one billion."

Technology and virtual reality—including our screens!—are quietly altering our understanding of reality itself. And in this transformation, the new forms of "screen entertainment" are up for grabs. Even the big brains of the business with huge fortunes at stake don't know how to bet on the future. The trends are growing too numerous and expanding too rapidly.

Tomorrow, we will suddenly see that *everything has changed*.

Embodied Minds

Even today, we can see why. We can see a convergence of historic events that are pulling the same "hair trigger." And the explosions have released the imagination, feeling, and power that flow from the world of nonliteral images and the call to participate.

This is not a game. And it is not for children. It is *serious make-believe*.

First, an overview:

This is the age of Virtual Reality. VR includes all the arts and is ʌthe first intellectual technology that permits the active use of the body in the search for knowledge.@[6] We are quickly migrating toward its virtual space.

Indeed, VR is not so virtual anymore. Companies are paying money for virtual real estate, and they are making money from virtual commerce. Surfers and gamers are spending real time—dozens of hours each week—in virtual environments. Couples are finding real love without having ever met. And our soldiers are playing video games with real results, flying real airplanes (drones) on the other side of the Earth and killing real people.

Of course, VR also brings blurring boundaries between "reality" and "virtual reality." It creates a fuzzy feedback loop between the actual and the imagined. We feel an increasing tension between fact and fiction, technology and art, real space and cyberspace, real time and "real time."

VR embeds itself in today's sensuous technologies where we live the duality of science and sense—the fusion of facts and feelings.

---

[6] Michael Heim, *Virtual Realism* (New York: Oxford University Press, 1998) pp. vii, viii.

Indeed, we are becoming cyborgs!—blending cyb(ernetics) with our org(anism).

The non-literal language of film and film music—with or without a computer—is becoming an integral part of our "embodied mind," for Virtual Reality is not possible without senses, feelings, and emotions.

A New "Knowing"

At the same time, Western Civilization has returned to an oral culture. In an oral culture, wisdom, history and meaning are pulled through the power of metaphor (story, ritual, pictures, dance, and song)—that is, through the power of the arts.

Today, it is a new way of "knowing." It is a knowing of the body. It is the aesthetic wisdom of the musing mind. It is the reflective thinking that flows from non-literal images. Perhaps more important, it is an "intuitive leap over the traditional step-by-step logical chain."[7]

And in an oral culture, art is *everything*. It is performance, it is meaning, and it is central to all understanding and memory. In a *literal* culture, on the other hand, the experience has been once removed by the representation of written language. Unless the language is poetry,

---

[7] Heim, 96.

the original event is reduced to mere letters on a page. Everything else is lost.

"Two-thirds of the world's population, either by necessity or choice, are already oral communicators, and they are found in every cultural group in the world."[8] For example, today's youth prefer a storied world over their mediocre and mundane literal world. With them, reality seems "like a poor substitute for the realms of the imagination."[9]

Even Tina Brown, former editor of the New Yorker, Vanity Fair and Newsweek, says she's "going back to oral culture where the written word will be less relevant."[10]

The Best Hope

Added to these epic events is "Postmodernism"—the secular story in which we all live.

---

[8] "Orality," Search.Com Reference, http://tinyurl.com/44puz58

[9] Pagan Kennedy's review of Gilsdorf, http://tinyurl.com/3zr4nyz

[10] "Tina Brown Slams Journalism, Says It's Having a 'Very, Very Pathetic Moment'" http://www.thewrap.com/tina-brown-magazines/

Radical and far-reaching, postmodernism simply says, "Don't listen to the opinions about 'right' and 'wrong' from people in positions of authority." "Doctrines—in whatever form—are out of style, so make up your own mind." For example, it's too late to tie today's youth to the last "official" answer. They're not interested. Consider, instead, how they review their reviewers—comment on their commentators—create shows about shows—read news commentary about news—follow TV guides about TV. They link, link, link, and their "evidence" becomes a simulation of a simulation of a simulation.

Of course, it's healthy to throw away worn-out ideas, but too many enthusiasts have "thrown the baby away with the bathwater." So Civilization desperately needs a new way to arrive at reality, meaning, and truth. Suddenly, the arts—including films—have become among the best hopes for a new way of "knowing."

Maybe a new way of "doing," as well. For advanced physics has proven we can change something simply by observing it. This may be the first scientific discovery of man's creativity. It also suggests that the arts may have a role in creating the future—that the arts were intended for far more than decoration or entertainment.

Taken together, Virtual Reality, Oral Culture, Postmodernism, and Advanced Physics promise a significant role for the future of Film—in one form or another. And if we remind ourselves that the word, "technology," which comes from the Greeks, means "the study of art," then we will surely fulfill that ancient prophecy.

A Rediscovered Metaphor

Unfortunately, we are not ready. Technology is expanding and accelerating the above trends beyond any institution's ability to understand, guide, or control. We stagger under a subject that seems strange, exotic, and even alien to traditional thinkers.

Yes, we know that music is expressive, that it has an emotional effect, that it offers some kind of intuitive evocation to the film, but "the 'how' continues to remain elusive."[11] Nevertheless, we will find the answer here.

Intellectuals have rediscovered a "metaphor" that lies beyond a mere figure of speech. In a language identical to the language of film and film music, this metaphor turns out to be the building block for all the arts,[12] the only hope for

---

[11] Jennifer Shipon, History of Music in Film: Analysis of How & Why Film Scores Enhance the Emotional Import of Films: *Citizen Kane* http://voices.yahoo.com/history-music-film-analysis-why-film-36641.html?cat=7

[12] Carl Hausman, *Metaphor and art: Interactionism and Reference in the Verbal and*

abstract thought,[13] and "the most fertile power possessed by man."[14]

Nonverbal Arts (New York: Cambridge University Press, 1989) pp. 5, 111, 198.

[13] Lakoff and Johnson, _Philosophy in the Flesh: The Embodied Mind and Its Challenge to Western Thought_ (New York, NY: Basic Books, 1999) pp. 58, 59.

[14] José Ortega y Gasset, _GoodReads,_ http://tinyurl.com/4xjuuoj

SUGGESTED JOURNEY

This book presents a series of suggested journeys with film music. We begin with the music to *Star Wars*:

Star Wars is a 1977 American, epic, space-opera film written and directed by George Lucas. In the film, a group of freedom fighters plot to destroy the powerful Death Star space station, a devastating weapon created by the evil Galactic Empire. This conflict disrupts the isolated life of farm boy Luke Skywalker when he inadvertently acquires the droids (robotic machines) carrying the stolen plans to the Death Star. After the Empire begins a cruel and destructive search for the droids, Skywalker decides to accompany Jedi Master Obi-Wan Kenobi on a daring mission to rescue the owner of the droids, rebel leader Princess Leia, and save the galaxy. (From an online summary.)

The music was written by John Williams (born 1932), an American composer and conductor. Many observers consider him our greatest film composer.

The main title theme can be found at several locations. Here is a suggested link: http://tinyurl.com/lcesy7j

Listen to the music, and answer the following questions. You may need to hear the music more than once. Your answers should point to a similar—though not exact—pattern of senses, feelings, and emotions as described in the story. In later chapters, we will explore the power of music to enhance the story of film.

1. While listening to this music, what sounds do you notice most? You don't have to be musically trained to answer. Just describe in your own words the general nature of the sounds you are hearing. These are simply "first impressions."

2. What particular sounds would you remember a week from now?

3. Describe the sounds you like the most. Why?

4. Describe the sounds you like the least. Why?

5. If you were the composer, what musical instruments or voices would you add? What kinds of musical sounds would you join with the sounds already there?

6. If you were an avant-garde composer and wanted to add non-musical sounds to this music, what would they be?

7. While this music is playing, describe your own picture that would match the music.

8. Complete the details of that picture.

9. What emotions are involved in the picture?

10. Give the picture a title.

11. Have you seen an event similar to this?

12. Have you experienced similar emotions? Describe.

13. If there is a "message" in this music, how would you reply?

II. A BRIEF HISTORY

From Silent Film to Sound Film

The Frenchman, Louis Lumiere, is often cited as the inventor in 1895 of the first motion picture camera. At that time, there was no sound. Only images.

Music with drama, however, had been around long before in opera, vaudeville, and other staged show-business. Even concert music, especially the romantic and melodramatic music of the nineteenth century, foreshadowed the music of later sound films. In other words, the long-awaited film music was already there.

Yet, the first films were entirely without sound, so "live" music became obviously needed to mimic the action of the film and to mask the distracting noise of the projection machine. Usually, talented pianists were hired by "picture houses" to improvise the differing moods demanded by the differing moments of silent movies. My mother Maye Waid was one of those early pianists.

In larger cities, orchestras filled the same role, but with borrowed sequences of classical music and sometimes trite inventions of Rolodex-type moods. Nevertheless, moments of a growing art appeared with early films like *The Birth of a Nation* (1914). And professional traveling orchestras performing unique quotations from classical scores accompanied the national tours of the latest films. As a young musician, I played some of these musical adaptations. They were so complexly cued that almost any size and combination of players could perform even epic masterworks from the symphonic repertoire.

The technique for talking sequences in the movie, *The Jazz Singer*, ushered in the era of "talkies" (sound films) in 1927. And *The Birth of a Nation* was the first movie with a musical score put together specifically for it.

Frustratingly Awkward

Increasing prestige for early film music came from more advanced composers like Honegger, Meisel, Milhaud, Ruttmann, and Shostakovich. Examples include *Battleship Potyomkin* (1925), *October* (1927), and the documentary *Berlin* (1927).

The development of musical technique for "talkies" was slow going, though. The skills for matching bits of music to a film were frustratingly awkward. In Germany, the first music that closely aligned itself with film appeared in Alfred Hitchcock's *Blackmail* (1929). The first notable progress, however, was *The Blue Angel,* composed by Friedrich Hollaender, and *The Brothers Karamazov*, composed by Karol Rathaus. The first USA pioneer of music for sound films was Max Steiner—an immigrant from Austria—who successfully fitted his music to David Selznick's film, *Symphony of Six Million* (1931).

Shortly after, Russian composers like Prokofiev, Shostakovich, Kabalevskky, and Shaporin; French composers like Milhaud, Auric, Honegger, and Maurice Jaubert; and English composers like Walter Leigh (*Song of Ceylon*), Britten, Bliss, Alwyn, Benjamin, Walton, Eisler, Korngold, and Antheil experimented successfully with music for the new sound films. By 1940, film music had come into its own.

In English films, Britain limited the composing of film music to respected "serious" composers. During the 1940s, the public heard film music by Ireland, Rawsthorne, Bax, Vaughan Williams, Malcolm Arnold, John Addison, William Alwyn, Clifton Parker, Elisabeth Lutyens, Benjamin Frankel, Anthony Collins, and Cedric Thorpe Davie. Especially notable are *Man of Aran* (1934) by John Greenwood, and *The Red Shoes* (1948) by Brian Easdale. Several years later, we can hear important work by Richard Rodney Bennett, Frank Cordell, Alfred Ralston, Laurie Johnson, and Ron Goodwin.

Early Hollywood composers, by contrast, were not part of the highly skilled European tradition. In the early years, some critics called them anonymous hacks, writing music that could have been written by anybody. We might understand why, for in the "golden years," Hollywood produced about 400 films a year, requiring fulltime, assembly-line "workmen."

Some of these composers, however, came from middle and eastern Europe, and their skillful romantic styles were practiced successfully by Max Steiner, Roy Webb, Alfred Newman, Dimitri Tiomkin, and Herbert Stothart. Later, the increased "realism" in film brought forth the music of Bernard Herrmann and Miklós Rózsa. Herrmann was especially known for the music to Orson Welles's *Citizen Kane* (1940) Other American exceptions to the European takeover of Hollywood's musical world were Aaron Copland, George Antheil, and Virgil Thomson.

"The Devil is in the Details"

The actual process of bonding the film's music with its drama has been far from perfect. Common sense suggests that—from the beginning—the film's composer and the film's director should work together. But the composer must usually wait until the film has already been shot and cut. Of course, this rules out artistic teamwork and forces the composer to fit his music into a "box" —the limited sequence and exact timing of the drama itself. The problem becomes obvious when music is taken from the film and performed on its own in a concert. The result is often a string of hacked audio clips—resembling a "string of sausages"— that cannot stand on their own.

In place of collaborating from the beginning, composers and directors looked for positive outcomes from an alternate process. Composers explain how they benefit from seeing the finished results of the film itself. And, by that time, the directors finally understand what they want from the music and finally share those intentions with the composer.

But the devil is in the details: (1) The music editor gives the exact timings of each film sequence to the composer. (2) Then, correct tempos are made "audible" with a "click track" and fed into the conductor's earphones. (3) At the same time, the conductor watches a screen behind the orchestra and looks for "white dots" that demand agreement with the film. (4) Added sound effects take priority over the music and the final cutting of the drama can easily ruin the intended effects of the music. (5) Often, more music is added or replaced in the original score by unknown hacks that have been hired without credit or permission from the original composer.

Endless Experiments

Some observers separate film music into two types: "functional" and "realistic." Realistic music mimics or replicates the drama as if it were an original part of the action. Functional music, on the other hand, interprets or translates the original drama into a separate art form. In other words, the music is once removed, yet deepens and widens the original inspiration. Unfortunately, some composers add mere incidental background or shallow atmosphere to the moment.

While the film's musical requirements, combined with the composers own style, usually provide the foundation for the final product, several composers have experimented with short musical motives for the main characters of the story. In turn, variations on these motives capture the changing themes of the drama itself. Examples include Vaughan Williams's *Scott of the Antarctic* (1948), Walton's *Henry V* (1944) and *Hamlet* (1948), Hermann's *Citizen Kane* (1940), Friedhofer's *Best Years of our Lives* (1946), North's *Cleopatra* (1962) and Elmer Bernstein's *The Great Escape* (1963).

Other experiments beyond the standard symphonic orchestra include different types and sizes of musical instruments, electronic sounds, and a variety of unorthodox sonorities in keeping with equally unorthodox visual elements.

The film composer finds additional challenge when setting music to premodern or even ancient stories, for the music of earlier times usually remain irrelevant to modern ears. The composer can only suggest the mood and style and, hopefully, avoid slipping into satire or parody.

Early on, the "opening credits" of a film gave the composer the liberty of writing music that set the tone, mood, and theme of the entire story. Later, the "closing credits" also provided film composers the opportunity to feature music uninterrupted by the necessities of dialogue, yet long enough to stand on its own, even when performed at concerts.

Though less easily manipulated, the classical music repertoire is sometimes welcomed *as is* by film directors. Nationalist documentaries often use the repertoire of their own nationalist composers. Or, when concert music and screen stories embrace the same subject they can be found in the same film. An example: the music from Delius's *Appalachia* and the film, *The Yearling* (1946); or Richard Strauss's *Also Sprach Zarathustra* and *2001---a Space Odyssey* (1968).

An unusual experiment comes from film makers who have reversed the whole film making process: adding visual images to already composed music. Examples include: Jean Mitry's *Pacific 231* (1949) and *Images pour Debussy* (1952), Renzo Avanzo's *Fountains of Rome* (1953) and Walt Disney's *Fantasia* (1940). In theory, this should be just as easy and inspiring as starting only with a script.

"Realistic music" is often part of the on-screen action, and when that action portrays previous cultures, music historians contribute to the film's research. For example, the study of Tahitian musicians and dancers contributed to the music of *Mutiny on the Bounty* (1962). And, early Greek and Hebrew modal melodies informed the music of *Quo vadis?* (1951).

Not So "Golden"

But there were major changes yet to come for Hollywood. Just a few years later, harsh harmonies, unrelenting jazz-like reverberations, and the absence of simple melodies permeated the music of Friedhofer's *Best Years of our Lives* (1946), Alex North's *A Streetcar Named Desire* (1951), and Leonard Rosenman's two significant achievements: *East of Eden* (1954) and *Rebel without a Cause* (1955).

During this time, even the music for Westerns was reinvented. Moross's score to *The Big Country* (1958) inspired Elmer Bernstein, John Williams, and Dominic Frontière.

Then came television, drawing audiences away from films and forcing the closure of the larger studio "music departments." Suddenly, composers were part of smaller, film-making teams and freed from the more controlled, preconceived musical products. On the positive side, this provided rare opportunities to combine the new and the old, the traditional and the experimental, the popular and the avant-garde. But studios also opted to save money by hiring second-rate talent and marketing their pop songs in the recordings that would come afterwards.

So for every creative breakthrough (the Beatles' *A Hard day's Night*, 1964, as example), there was just as much stagnant backwater marketing.

Encouraging Nevertheless

Nevertheless, today's movie music is finally a respected study at leading universities, and the music is often written by serious concert composers. These composers include Toru Takemitsu, Peter Maxwell Davies, Andre Previn, Elliott Goldenthal, Alfred Schnittke, Leonard Rosenman, John Corigliano, Steven Sondheim, Tan Dun, Phillip Glass, Steve Reich, Paul Chihara, William Bolcom, Rachel Portman, Paul Chihara, Hans Zimmer, Alan Menken, and others.

The history of film and film music is covered in several excellent sources.[1] The purpose of the present study, however, focuses more on "how" music adds to the profundity of a film. Nevertheless, we will finish this chapter with a list of the most important movie music—important either historically or artistically. This list covers 100 years between 1914 and 2014 and includes mostly English language films.

---

[1] Oxford Music Online & Grove Music Online, http://www.oxfordmusiconline.com.ezproxy.utpb.edu/subscriber/article/grove/music/09647?q=film+music&search=quick&source=omo_gmo&pos=1&_start=1

Note below how the list divides into decades. The reader will also want to remember Hollywood's "Golden Age" (1927 to 1963).[2] This is the "classical" Hollywood cinema period which refers to the visual and sound style unique to the American film industry of the time. This style—also called the "invisible" style—never calls attention to the camera or musical recording as they often did in previous periods, other countries, or in modern and postmodern art.

The American Film Institute's list of the "25 Greatest Film Scores of All Time" (1933 – 1986) is marked with an asterisk (*). And their top 10 list is marked with two asterisks (**).

Notice in this list your favorite films and see if you can also remember the music. If you can't remember the music, Classical Hollywood might say that's a good sign.

---

[2] Goldburg, Michael. "Classical Hollywood Cinema"
http://faculty.washington.edu/mlg/courses/defi nitions/classicalHollywoodcinema.html

IMPORTANT FILMS FROM 1914 TO 2014

1914:

The Birth of a Nation (1914) Joseph Carl Breil

1920's

Battleship Potyomkin (1925) Nikolai Kryukov

Don Juan (1926) Axt/Mendosa

The Jazz Singer (1927) Louis Silvers

Blackmail (1929) Campbell, Connelly, Mayerl

The Broadway Melody (1929)
Herb/Brown/Cohan/Robison

Sous les toits de Paris (1929)
Bernard/Moretti/Nazelles

Petite Lili (1929) Darius Milhaud

Black and Tan (1929) Duke Ellington

St Louis Blues (1929) W. C. Handy

1930's

The King of Jazz (1930) Paul Whiteman
Orchestra

FILM MUSIC

Sunny Side Up (1930) Earl Burtnett, Johnny Hamp, & others

The Blue Angel (1930 & 1959) Hollaender/Waxman

Der blaue Engel (1930) Karol Rathaus

Alone (1930) Sergei Shostakovich

Symphony of Six Million (1931) Max Steiner

Le sang d'un poète (1931) Georges Auric

The Brothers Karamazov (1931) Karol Rathaus

Vampyr (1932) Wolfgang Zeller

Rhapsody in Black and Blue (1932) Louis Armstrong

Gold Diggers (1933) Busby Berkeley

Lieutenant Kijé (1933) Sergei Shostakovich

*King Kong (1933) Max Steiner

Deserter (1933) Yury Shaporin

Little Women (1933) Max Steiner

Song of Ceylon (1934) Walter Leigh

Man of Aran (1934) John Greenwood

Top Hat, 1935) Irving Berlin

Captain Blood (1935) Erich Korngold

Symphony in Black (1935) Duke Ellington

Roberta (1935) Max Steiner/Jerome Kern

The Informer (1935) Max Steiner

The Bride of Frankenstein (1935) Franz Waxman

Swing Time (1936) Jerome Kern

Anthony Adverse (1936) Erich Korngold

The Plow that Broke the Plains (1936) Virgil Thomson

The Plainsman (1937) George Antheil

Shall we Dance, (1937) George Gershwin

**Gone With the Wind* (1938) Max Steiner

The Adventures of Robin Hood (1938) Erich Korngold

Pygmalion (1938) Honegger

Aleksandr Nevsky (1938) Sergei Prokofiev

The Wizard of Oz (1939) Arlen/Stothart

1940's

The Sea Hawk (1940) Erich Korngold

Fantasia (1940) Various concert works

Rebecca (1940) Franz Waxman

Of Mice and Men (1940) Aaron Copland

Our Town (1940) Aaron Copland

Citizen Kane (1940) Bernard Herrmann

Suspicion (1941) Franz Waxman

The Devil and Daniel Webster (1941) Bernard Herrmann

Now Voyager (1942) Max Steiner

Casablanca (1942) Max Steiner

Kings Row (1942) Eric Korngold

The Magnificent Ambersons (1942) Bernard Bernard Herrmann

Jammin' the Blues (1944) Several jazz musicians

Double Indemnity (1944) Miklós Rózsa

Farewell my Lovely (1944) Roy Webb

Ivan the Terrible (Two parts: 1944 and 1946) Sergei Prokofiev

**Laura* (1944) David Raksin

Henry V (1944) William Walton

Spellbound (1945) Miklós Rózsa

The Lost Weekend (1945) Dimitri Tiomkin

The Spiral Staircase (1945) Roy Webb

Rhapsody in Blue (1945) George Gershwin

The Crimson Canary (1945) Leading jazz musicians

Of Human Bondage (1946) Erich Korngold

Best Years of our Lives (1946) Hugo Friedhofer

The Yearling (1946) Michael Leonard

The Fabulous Dorseys (1947) The Dorsey Brothers

The Lost Moment (1947) Daniele Amfitheatrof

The Secret beyond the Door (1948) Miklós Rózsa

The Red Shoes (1948) Brian Easdale

Force of Evil (1948) David Raksin

The Treasure of the Sierra Madre (1948) Max Steiner

The Bicycle Thief (1948) Alessandro Cicognini

Macbeth (1948) Jacques Ibert

Scott of the Antarctic (1948) Vaughan Williams

Hamlet (1948) William Walton

The Red Pony (1949) Aaron Copland

The Heiress (1949) Aaron Copland

Young Man with a Horn (1949) Harry James

Pinky (1949) Alfred Newman

Passport to Pimlico (1949) Georges Auric

The Fall of Berlin (1949) Dmitri Shostakovich

The Battle of Stalingrad (1949) Aram Khachaturian

Pacific 231 (1949) Arthur Honegger

1950's

Sunset Boulevard (1950) Franz Waxman

Panic in the Streets (1950) Alfred Newman

Quo vadis? (1951) Miklós Rózsa

The Unforgettable Year 1919 (1951) Dmitri Shostakovich

The Day the Earth Stood Still (1951) Bernard Herrmann

The Lavender Hill Mob (1951) Georges Auric

Quo vadis? (1951) Miklós Rózsa

*A Streetcar Named Desire (1951) Alex North

**High Noon (1952) Dimitri Tiomkin

Images pour Debussy (1952) Claude Debussy

Fountains of Rome (1953) Renzo Avanzo

Tokyo Story (1953) Kojun Saito

The Wild One (1953) Leith Stevens

The Robe (1953) Alfred Newman

Julius Caesar (1953) Miklós Rózsa

The Glenn Miller Story (1954) Miller/Gershenson/Mancini

*On the Waterfront (1954) Leonard Bernstein

East of Eden (1955) Leonard Rosenman

Rebel without a Cause (1955) Leonard Rosenman

The Cobweb (1955) Leonard Rosenman

The Man with the Golden Arm (1955) Elmer Bernstein

The Blackboard Jungle (1955) Max Freedman

The Gadfly (1955) Dmitri Shostakovich

Animal Farm (1955) Matyas Seiber

Kurutta kajitsu (1956) Tōru Takemitsu

Forbidden Planet (1956) Louis and Bebe Barron

Rock around the Clock (1956) Max Freedman

Love me Tender (1956) Lionel Newman

Giant (1956) Dimitri Tiomkin

Friendly Persuasion (1956) Dimitri Tiomkin

Crime in the Streets (1956) Franz Waxman

The Benny Goodman Story (1956) Gershenson/Mancini & others

Loving You (1957) Walter Scharf

Jailhouse Rock (1957) Jeff Alexander

Sait-on jamais (1957) John Lewis

The Bridge on the River Kwai (1957) Malcolm Arnold

St Louis Blues (1958) W. C. Handy & others

I Want to Live! (1958) Johnny Mandel

Touch of Evil (1958) Henry Mancini

L'ascenseur pour l'échafaud (1958) Miles Davis

Black Orpheus (1958) Bonfa, Carlos, and Gilberto

FILM MUSIC

The Big Country (1958) Jerome Moross

**Vertigo (*1958) Bernard Bernard Herrmann

The Brothers Karamazov (1958) Karol Rathaus

The Gene Krupa Story (1959) Leith Stevens

Odds against Tomorrow (1959) John Lewis

Anatomy of a Murder (1959) Duke Ellington

Shadows (1959) Charles Mingus, Curtis Porter

Look Back in Anger (1959) Chris Barber

Expresso Bongo (1959) Monty Norman, David Heneker

North by Northwest (1959) Bernard Bernard Herrmann

*Ben-Hur (1959) Miklós Rózsa

1960's

**Magnificent Seven (1960) Elmer Bernstein

**Psycho (1960) Bernard Herrmann

Spartacus (1960) Alex North

King of Kings (1961) Miklós Rózsa

Paris Blues (1961) Duke Ellington

El Cid (1961) Miklós Rózsa

The Innocents (1961) Georges Auric

Breakfast at Tiffany's (1961) Henry Mancini

Paris Blues (1961) Duke Ellington

*To Kill a Mockingbird (1962) Elmer Bernstein

**Lawrence of Arabia (1962) Maurice Jarre

How the West Was Won (1962) Alfred Newman & Ken Darby

Sanjuro (1962) Kojun Saito

Cleopatra (1962) Alex North

Mutiny on the Bounty (1962) Bronisław Kaper

Tom Jones (1963) John Addison

Summer Holiday (1963) Black, Myers, & Cass

The Servant (1963) John Dankworth

Cleopatra (1963) Alex North

The Birds (1963) Bernard Herrmann

The Great Escape (1963) Elmer Bernstein

633 Squadron (1964) Ron Goodwin

A Fistful of Dollars (1964) Ennio Morricone

A Hard Day's Night (1964) The Beatles & George Martin

The Umbrellas of Cherbourg (1964) Michel Legrand

The Pink Panther (1964) Henry Mancini

The Gospel according to St Matthew (1964) Luis Enriquez Bacalov

Zorba the Greek (1964) Mikis Theodorakis

Hamlet (1964) Dmitri Shostakovich

The Woman of the Dunes (1964) Tōru Takemitsu

Doctor Zhivago (1965) Maurice Jarre

For a Few Dollars More (1965) Ennio Morricone

Fantastic Voyage (1966) Leonard Rosenman

The Blue Max (1966) Jerry Goldsmith

The Good, The Bad and the Ugly (1966) Ennio Morricone

A Man Called Adam (1966) Benny Carter

Blow-Up (1966) Herbie Hancock

Alfie (1966) Sonny Rollins

Peter Gunn (1967) Henry Mancini

Sweet Love Bitter (1967) Mal Waldron

The Odd Couple (1967) Neal Nefti

In Cold Blood (1967) Quincy Jones

The Graduate (1967) Simon and Garfunkel/ Dave Grusin

2001---a Space Odyssey (1968) Various concert works

Planet of the Apes (1968) Jerry Goldsmith

Bullitt (1968) Lalo Schifrin

Head (1968) Ken Thorne

Butch Cassidy and the Sundance Kid (1969) Burt Bacharach

Easy Rider (1969) Roger McGuinn

Zabriskie Point (1969) Pink Floyd & Jerry Garcia

Airport (1969) Alfred Newman

True Grit (1969) Elmer Bernstein

Where Eagles Dare (1969) Ron Goodwin

Once upon a Time in the West (1969) Ennio Morricone

1970's

Jack Johnson (1970) Miles Davis

King Lear (1970) Dmitri Shostakovich

A Clockwork Orange (1971) Giorgio Moroder

Summer of '42 (1971) Michel Legrand

Straw Dogs (1971) Jerry Fielding

**Godfather* (1972) Nino Rota

Lady Sings the Blues (1972) Michel Legrand & Gil Askey

Sisters (1972) Bernard Herrmann

Jesus Christ Superstar (1973) <u>Webber</u>, Previn, & Spencer

The Way we Were (1973) Marvin Hamlisch

American Graffiti (1973) "41 original hits" (no soundtrack)

The Exorcist (1973) Jack Nitzsche

***Chinatown* (1974) Jerry Goldsmith

Death Wish (1974) Herbie Hancock

***Jaws* (1975) John Williams

Taxi Driver (1976) Bernard Herrmann

The Omen (1976) Jerry Goldsmith

***Star Wars* (1977) John Williams

New York, New York (1977) John Kander & Fred Ebb

Saturday Night Fever (1977) Barry, Robin, & Maurice Gibb

Sorcerer (1977) The Group, Tangerine Dream

Midnight Express (1978) Giorgio Moroder

Halloween (1978) John Carpenter

The Silent Partner (1978) Oscar Petersen

Grease (1978) Jacobs, Casey, & Gibson

The Lord of the Rings (1978) Rosenman

Hair (1979) Galt MacDermot

Star Trek: the Motion Picture (1979) Jerry Goldsmith

1980's

Chariots of Fire (1981) Vangelis

*On Golden Pond (1981) Dave Grusin

Thief (1981) The Group, Tangerine Dream

Raiders of the Lost Ark (1981) John Williams

*E.T. (1982) John Williams

Koyaanisqatsi (1983) Philip Glass

Videodrome (1983) Howard Shore

The Company of Wolves (1984) George Fenton

Beverly Hills Cop (1984) Faltermeyer/ Elfman

The Cotton Club (1984) John Barry

The Falcon and the Snowman (1984) Mays & Metheny

The Killing Fields (1984) Mike Oldfield

Paris, Texas (1984) Ry Cooder

Once upon a Time in America (1984) Ennio Morricone

Runaway (1985) Jerry Goldsmith

*Out of Africa (1985) John Barry

*The Mission (1986) Ennio Morricone

Round Midnight (1986) Herbie Hancock

Top Gun (1986) Harold Faltermeyer

Legend (1986) Jerry Goldsmith & Tangerine Dream

Fatal Attraction (1987) Maurice Jarre

Powaqqatsi (1988) Philip Glass

Bird (1988) Lennie Niehaus

Criminal Law (1988) Jerry Goldsmith

The Fabulous Baker Boys (1989) Dave Grusin

Casualties of War (1989) Ennio Morricone

1990's

Mo' Better Blues (1990) Bill Lee

La double vie de Véronique (1991) Zbigniew Preisner

Peter's Friends, (1992) Various artists

Bram Stoker's Dracula (1992) Wojciech Kilar

The Lion King (1993) Hans Zimmer

Rising Sun (1993) Tōru Takemitsu

Schindler's List (1993) John Williams

FILM MUSIC

Trois couleurs (1993–4) Zbigniew Preisner

Four Weddings and a Funeral (1994) Richard Rodney Bennett

Death and the Maiden (1995) Wojciech Kilar

The Portrait of a Lady (1996) Wojciech Kilar

Evita (1996) Andrew Lloyd Webber

William Shakespeare's Romeo and Juliet (1996) Hooper, Vries, & Armstrong

The Secret Agent (1996) Philip Glass

2000's

The Legend of Bagger Vance (2000) Rachel Portman

Harry Potter and the Sorcerer's Stone (2001) John Williams

The Lord of the Rings: The Fellowship of the Ring (2001) Howard Shore, Enya

The Mists of Avalon (TV) (2001) Lee Holdridge

Frida (2002) Elliot Goldenthal

The Lord of the Rings: The Two Towers (2002) Howard Shore

Star Wars: Attack of the Clones (2002) John Williams

Angels in America (TV) (2003) Thomas Newman

Children of Dune (TV) (2003) Brian Tyler

Gods and Generals (2003) John Frizzell, Randy Edelman

The Gospel of John (2003) Jeff Danna

The Lord of the Rings: The Return of the King (2003) Howard Shore

The Missing (2003) James Horner

Sinbad: Legend of the Seven Seas (2003) Harry Gregson-Williams

Timeline (2003) Brian Tyler, Jerry Goldsmith

Alexander (2004) Vangelis

Arsène Lupin (2004) Debbie Wiseman

Deep Blue (2004) George Fenton

The Terminal (2004) John Williams

Troy (2004) James Horner, Gabriel Yared

The Brothers Grimm (2005) Dario Marianelli

The Legend of Zorro (2005) James Horner

Racing Stripes (2005) Mark Isham

Lady in the Water (2006) James Newton Howard

The Nativity Story (2006) Mychael Danna

The Promise (2006) Klaus Badelt

Superman Returns (2006) John Ottman

Angel (2007) Philippe Rombi

Curse of the Golden Flower (2006) Shigeru Umebayashi

Island of Lost Souls (2007) Jane Antonia Cornish

Nomad: The Warrior (2007) Carlo Siliotto

Agora (2009) Dario Marianelli

Avatar (2009) James Horner

Pope Joan (Die Päpstin) (2009) Marcel Barsotti

2010's

Alice in Wonderland (2010) Danny Elfman

The Chronicles of Narnia: The Voyage of the Dawn Treader (2010) David Arnold

The Last Airbender (2010) James Newton Howard

The Adventures of Tintin: The Secret of the Unicorn (2011) John Williams

La Ligne Droite (2011) Patrick Doyle

Priest (2011) Christopher Young

Real Steel (2011) Danny Elfman

Soul Surfer (2011) Marco Beltrami

The Hobbit: An Unexpected Journey (2012)
Howard Shore

Journey 2: The Mysterious Island (2012)
Andrew Lockington

The Hobbit: The Desolation of Smaug (2013)
Howard Shore

Jack the Giant Slayer (2013) John Ottman

Now You See Me (2013) Brian Tyler

Romeo & Juliet (2013) Abel Korzeniowski

SUGGESTED JOURNEY

Citizen Kane is an American film drama written in 1941. Orson Welles played not only the starring role, he also helped write and produce this masterpiece. Many critics and film producers consider it the greatest of all films. In fact, it was voted the greatest film in five Sight & Sound's critics' polls, until Vertigo displaced it in a 2012 poll. Its cinematography, narrative structure, and music have been especially recognized as historic breakthroughs for their time.

Typical of the time, the composer Bernard Hermann was trained in Germany. Hermann wrote the music to almost one hundred film scores. We have presented below the music from *Citizen Kane*. After listening to the music [http://tinyurl.com/p7fruqv] and reading the plot summaries [http://tinyurl.com/ncyjp98] describe the two main moods in this musical excerpt from the film. What does the juxtaposition of these opposing moods point to in the movie? How do these mood-juxtapositions reveal the ultimate significance of the story itself?

III. WHAT IS FILM MUSIC?

Suspending Disbelief

So what is film music? It's surprising how few have a clue. Usually, we narrow the idea of film music to "music that accompanies a movie." And, true enough, that expresses the limit of much film music.

We take it for granted. After all, logical thinking requires focusing on one thing at a time. In this case, it is usually the film narrative. Everything else must support and be subservient to the film. In other words, "the music must always accompany the movie." The notion that film music could differ from or even "oppose" the film flies in the face of informed thought.

We will see, though, that the language of film music is the *language of juxtaposition* where things are put together that don't necessarily go together. They can even oppose each other! Remember in the first chapter the distinguished observer who claimed that the concept of film music is "bizarre"? Further, this language of juxtaposition requires an *intuitive* response that—unlike logical thinking—easily grasps endless juxtaposed subjects in the same moment.

So our definition of "Film Music" will require a difficult suspension of disbelief.

As Samuel Taylor Coleridge asserted nearly two hundred years ago, the enjoyment of art depends on the audience's "willing suspension of disbelief."[1] This suspension—the "buy-in" of the tension between the known and the unknown or the relevant and the irrelevant—allows us to enjoy everything from *The Divine Comedy* to *Star Wars*.

Therefore, let us begin with this definition of Film Music:

> Film music is the ***intuitive, nonliteral*** language of ***juxtaposition***. Using the sense of sound, participation in this language is ***immersive*** and ***interactive***, and the result of the experience is ***felt meaning***.

Each of the above terms deserves its own description:

---

[1] Neil Greenberg, *Art And Organism: A Biological Perspective on Art and Aesthetics* http://tinyurl.com/69ekj8z

IV. FILM MUSIC IS INTUITIVE

If you must explain a joke, it's not funny. True enough. We can always observe, examine, and analyze events, but intuition happens **before** we figure it out. In other words, it is a spur-of-the-moment knowing that sees hidden links between things. We could even call it a trans-rational awareness since it ignores "the traditional step-by-step logical chain."[2]

We often describe an "aha" moment as a gut feeling, an inkling, or a hunch. Sometimes we report, "It came to me out of the clear blue sky." Or, consider this example:

> An NFL quarterback has to make several hard decisions in a few seconds before he is crushed. Every play is a mixture of careful planning and risky split-second improvisation. How does he make all the decisions? It's as if his mind is making decisions without him![3]

---

[2] Heim, 96.

[3] Jonah Lehrer, quoted in David May's book review of *How We Decide*, (Orlando, FL: Houghton Mifflin Harcourt, 2009) http://tinyurl.com/6x2uot3

Few are quarterbacks, but all of us need this gift. The intuitive mind functions on a level with far more sensitivity and complexity than that of well-ordered thought.

> You cannot study Pleasure in the moment of nuptial embrace . . . nor analyze the nature of humor while roaring with laughter.[4]

In short, we cannot do without the intuitive revelation that is birthed from profound inspiration and that comes from beyond ordinary knowledge or intelligence.

---

[4] C. S. Lewis quoted in:
http://tinyurl.com/6ev57gf

V. FILM MUSIC IS NONLITERAL

Film music is also nonliteral. It moves beyond "structured" communication. It stands free of our semantic rulebooks, and it snubs the precision of language twisted to its own devices.

In other words, film music is **extralinguistic**.

It composes its own rubrics, leaping beyond past pomposity and revealing meaning outside our bound dictionaries. Rather than an enlightened march toward the last "correct" answer, film music enjoys the feelings of meaningful mosaics or the kaleidoscope of prescient patterns.

The ancient Hebrews knew this: "In many separate revelations [each of which set forth a portion of the Truth] and in different ways God spoke of old to [our] forefathers in and by the prophets."[1] In other words, the Hebrews welcomed all revelations yet knew them as "portions" of one Truth. In the same way, film music reveals multiple insights of one underlying theme. Language serves no purpose to modern minds if it has no clarity or

---

[1] Hebrews 1:1, *The Amplified Bible* (Grand Rapids, MI: Zondervan Corporation, 1987).

conciseness. Yet, film music torments us. It half-unveils and half-vanishes. It deliberately disguises. It becomes **intentionally** vague. Not providing answers is just as vital as providing answers. After all, how else can it be both nonliteral and intuitive?

It's obvious then that both film and film music are essentially sentient languages—involving the senses, feelings, and emotions—for they depend on a "pre-semantic surface of human experience for its power."[2]

The grammar experts call anything "nonliteral" a figure of speech. And, no doubt, expert writers winningly manipulate their figurative materials. Too often, though, the fleeting emptiness of shallow yet colorful words and the uninspired clichés of dead metaphors fail to create the film masterpieces of our time. In our "enlightened" thinking, we have lost the profundity of metaphor—whether in words or music. The ancient Hebrews, for example, believed prophetic metaphor to be the very voice of God.[3]

---

[2] Lewis Edwin Hahn, Editor, *The Philosophy of Paul Ricoeur* (Chicago: Open Court, 1995) p. 216.

[3] Hosea explains in 12:10 that God speaks to us through *damah*, meaning "prophetic metaphor."

We should at least remember the gifts of the right-brain with its powers of pattern recognition, holistic perceptions, emotions, feelings, and intuition. And we should at least admit that language dies in order to live, and that today's language is less about literal words. Indeed, we are living in a "postliterate era."[4]

Hence, the utter necessity of the arts.

The transparent tensions within film and film music may become our only passport to a not-so-fictional reality. The "language of juxtaposition" provides access to that world.

It comes next.

---

[4] Ryan, 60, 61.

VI. FILM MUSIC IS THE "LANGUAGE OF JUXTAPOSITION"

Opposing Faces

Film music must do more than simply add to the atmosphere, provide continuity, intensify the action, or decrease its intensity. It must do more than merely mimic the truisms of the story. And it must do more than only add to the eye-candy extravagance or hell-bent action of the visual spectacle.

Music provides an equally powerful, equally extraordinary perception that births from a language separate from that of film. Though music easily acquiesces to accompanying, it was never meant to provide a "supporting role." That's because its language is *juxtaposition*— placing two things together that don't go together, the tension of which points to a third reality beyond the juxtaposition itself.

There's no "accompanying" here.

The ancient Greeks and Hebrews believed in a poetic and prophetic force called *prosopon*, meaning "a face facing a face." Further, they believed the resulting tensions between opposing faces finally point to a third reality or radical otherness, which they called the *Geist*, *pneuma*, or "Spirit of Truth."

So the strange relationship between film and film music affects us most when their supposed agreement is totally unknown yet ultimately "so wonderfully knowable."[1] Their friendship, in other words, is a half-unveiling, half-vanishing act. And the show stops when the unveiled side totally unveils (as in accompanying) or the vanishing side totally vanishes (as in the complete destruction of their relationship).

Both within and between film and film music, the "known" launches us into the "unknown," while the "unknown" finds anchor in the "known." The "known" brings body to the "unknown," while the "unknown" adds power to the "known."

The Secret Grief of the Happy Clown

In a serious, make-believe realm, both film and film music create tensions between the known and the unknown, the real and the unreal, the expected and the unexpected. They hold cheek by jowl the old and the new, the local and the global, this world and another world. And they juxtapose the beautiful and the ugly, the

---

[1] Dudley Andrew "Cinema & Culture" *Humanities*, Vol. 6, No. 4 (August 1985), pp. 24-25

ordinary and the odd, the force of habit and the shock of the new.

In the ancient metaphor, "Time flies," we know "time"—the passing of days, for example—and we know "flight"—the wonder of birds, for example. But how these two "known" experiences can be put together remains "unknown." No matter how much you paraphrase and analyze it, the tension in this metaphor remains a mystery. Our brief moment on earth is more than logical observation. It takes our breath away.

It is the measure of our own mortality.

The unresolved tensions in these ridiculous rapports are like violin strings anchored at one end and cinched up at the other, rejoicing and suffering at the same time from the traveling bow. In a similar way, these radically different realities are like the archer's bow that propels its intentional arrow because of the tautness between the bow's opposing poles.

Sometimes wrestling, sometimes merely flirting, we've felt these opposing forces. We've sensed, for example, the carnival-like violations in the secret grief of the happy clown. We've wondered at Negro spirituals that sing of joy and sorrow at the same time. And we've tasted, concurrently, both sweetness and bitterness at a daughter's wedding.

Sometimes subtle, often not, these tensions break into our reality. These gaps in our knowledge strip the veil of familiarity from our world. They catch us off-guard, violate our expectations, and impertinently push our envelopes. They are "post-predictable."[2]

"Multi-Everything"

And, not surprisingly, they surprise us. Like alerted animals, we feel a quickening—an increased acuity of the senses—an instant focus. And we wait with an intense yearning for some kind of resolution. The more willing among us, however, meet these intrusions with the fascination and the excitement of a new journey. They're ready to "get somewhere." They know this is not the end. It's only the beginning.

The juxtapositions in music-drama are just the opposite from "good" thinking where thoughts narrow quickly to a single conclusion. For the tensions within these and other arts begin and end with "multi-everything."

To begin, they are *multimedia*. They take many forms. Not only can they masquerade as

---

[2] Chip Heath and Dan Heath, *Made to Stick: Why Some Ideas Survive and Others Die* (New York: Random House, 2007) p. 71.

sounds, movements, stories, images and anything else, they can also take place anytime and anywhere. A story, for example, "can be retold an infinite number of ways."[3]

Juxtaposition is also *multisensory* where one sense crosses easily to another sense: "The soprano has a 'sweet' voice." (Taste to hearing.) "The violinist has a 'velvet' tone." (Touch to hearing.) There is "no limit on the number of possible actualizations."[4]

They are also *multi-perspective*. Single juxtapositions pile on top of each other in fathomless complexity. These tumults of tensions become kaleidoscopic, and they do this on several levels at once. Though the notion remains unpopular among enlightened intellectuals, "Consciousness can occupy multiple points and points of view."[5] This gift means the film arts are a never-ending cycle of expanding resources, a constant state of flux and form, a whirling, revolving self-reflection of multifariousness. And this is their secret!

The more complex, the more tense; the more tense, the more meaning.

---

[3] Ryan, 119.

[4] Ryan, (above).

[5] Ryan, 71.

Music, for example, is a virtual skyscraper of juxtapositions with seemingly endless levels of tensions. Melodies go against their own directions; harmonies go against their own tonalities; rhythms interrupt their own beats, and the other elements of music (timbre, texture, form, dynamics, context, mood, and so forth) create similar ongoing tensions and resolutions of tensions. These tensions in music play not only within each element, but between each of the elements as well.

If all of those tensions were not enough, consider film. We have long searched for the powerful interface, the totalizing approach between all the arts. First, we called it drama (among the ancient Greeks), then opera . . . operetta . . . musical theater, and finally, motion pictures. Here, we find endless kaleidoscopes within endless kaleidoscopes when music, drama, visual art, narrative, and choreography work in amazing complexity—not only within each art form, but against each art form as well—to achieve a transcendent unifying principle.

The Very Seed of Art

The language of juxtaposition presents both the power and hope for music-drama. Great thinkers agree: Johann-Georg Hamann insisted, "Truth appears only through . . . contradictions of reason."[6] And Søren Kierkegaard echoed, "All existential truth is paradoxical . . . (and) the language of revelation . . . (is) absolute paradox."[7]

Perhaps it is helpful to identify juxtaposition with a *profound* metaphor—not a *literal* metaphor or a mere figure of speech. Admittedly, a literal metaphor "accomplishes in a word or phrase what could otherwise be expressed only in many words, if at all."[8] But great films and great film music are the "if at all."

Juxtaposition simply does not work if it follows the path of shallow metaphors that point only to themselves. Too much of the "known," for example, results in boredom—the tedium of clichés and dead metaphors. In other words, juxtaposition loses its power when the contradictions lose their power.

---

[6] Johann Georg Hamann, quoted in Louis Dupré, *Symbols of the Sacred* (Grand Rapids: Eerdmans, 2000) p. 58.

[7] Søren Kierkegaard, quoted in Dupré, p. 58.

[8] Elyse Sommer & Dorrie Weiss, *Metaphors Dictionary, First Edition* (Tampa, FL: International Thomson Publishing Company, 1995) p vii.

In the same way, too much of the "unknown" results in chaos—the total violation of the ordinary and the surreal distortions of life itself. "If you change (an apple) too much, it is no longer an apple."[9]

But great artists of all kinds recognize a profound metaphor that functions like our language of juxtaposition. Indeed, art is impossible without this kind of metaphor. It "represents the very structure of art . . . a perfect model of art." It is a miniature work of art, the very seed of art, a tiny portion of art. More important, it is the prototype and power in all the arts.[10]

But how do we participate in this power?

Whether creating or simply interpreting films or film music, we speak to the object of our attention in the language of juxtaposition. We create new juxtapositions that explore the continuities and connections that remain hidden in the original sensory image. And, again, we interface the unalike. We compare things that

---

[9] Cline, 102.

[10] Carl Hausman, *Metaphor and Art: Interactionism and Reference in the Verbal and Nonverbal Arts* (New York: Cambridge University Press, 1989) p 231.

---

cannot be compared, sometimes holding side-by-side other art forms and other senses.

Aristotle insisted, "The greatest thing by far is to be a master of metaphor."[11] With Greek and Hebrew artists/prophets, that meant inspired skill with the language of juxtaposition. We still need "the fascination with the discontinuous, the analogical jumps, the chance encounters of juxtapositions, and the back-blowing explosions caused by the collisions of juxtapositions."[12]

We see now that great film scores must translate the original inspiration of the film into a separate but parallel world. For the juxtaposition between film and film music is neither the candle nor the wick . . . .

. . . but the burning.

---

[11] Aristotle, *The Poetics*, http://tinyurl.com/3wfxf7m

[12] Ryan, 353.

SUGGESTED JOURNEY

The Pink Panther demonstrates the wide variety of film music styles and the often important inclusion of jazz. This film story is a comedy describing the deeds of the bumbling Inspector Clouseau, who must unravel the murder of a famed soccer coach and discover, as well, the thief of the notorious Pink Panther diamond.

The music is by Henry Mancini (1924 – 1994), an American composer, conductor and arranger, who is well-known for his film and television scores. His impressive career includes four Academy Awards, a Golden Globe, and ten Grammy Awards. He also received a posthumous Grammy Lifetime Achievement Award in 1995.

Before responding to the following questions, please recall our definition of Film Music:

"Film Music is the intuitive, nonliteral language of juxtaposition. Using the sense of sound, participation in this language is immersive and interactive, and the result of the experience is felt meaning."

Listen to the music and record your reflections:

[http://tinyurl.com/auuf927]

1. While listening to this music, what sounds do you notice most? Again, you don't have to be musically trained to answer this question. Just describe in your own words the general nature

of the sounds you are hearing. These are simply "first impressions."

2. What particular sounds would you remember a week from now?

3. Describe the sounds you like the most. Why?

4. Describe the sounds you like the least. Why?

5. If you were the composer, what musical instruments or voices would you add? What kinds of musical sounds would you join with the sounds already there?

6. If you were an avant-garde composer and wanted to add non-musical sounds to this music, what would they be?

7. While this music is playing, describe your own picture that would match the music.

8. Complete the details of that picture.

9. What emotions are involved in the picture?

10. Give the picture a title.

11. Have you seen an event similar to this?

12. Have you experienced similar emotions? Describe.

13. If there is a "message" in this music, how would you reply?

VII. FILM MUSIC IS IMMERSIVE

Caught Up in Another "Reality"

Film music requires the phenomenon of immersion. It happens when we feel "immersed" in a virtual time and place, when we feel absorbed in a different "world," or when our senses are caught up in another "reality."

In other words, immersion collapses the distinction between real and imagined worlds. It is a "first person" experience where we no longer look in from the outside, but look out from the inside. And, perhaps, it is always the initiation of the uninitiated.

Immersion also implies a fertile sensory involvement. It is the awareness of an **embodied** mind. It happens when our senses and feelings are captivated, engrossed, taken in—when they are moved, impelled, transported. Today's youth would call it being "in the zone" or "in the moment." It's like the almost total sensory involvement of reading books or playing video games, but . . .

> . . . at its best, immersion can be an adventurous and invigorating experience comparable to taking a swim in a cool ocean with powerful surf. The environment appears at first hostile, you

enter it reluctantly, but once you get wet and entrust your body to the waves, you never want to leave. And when you finally do, you feel refreshed and full of energy.[1]

Many fear immersion, though, for it seems to threaten critical thinking. And still others fear "getting lost"—the psychological dangers to the "self." These conversations come later. . . .

For now, simply recall that all of us continually live and "lose" ourselves in fictional worlds, not only in our ever-active imaginations and reflections, but in our choice of entertainment as well. Some of these experiences are certainly silly—"I can't believe I'm getting caught up in this"—and some are intentionally serious, for immersion is the goal of all great art.

Whenever and wherever, though, immersion should always be a conscious choice. Then, having made that choice, the embodied mind enters this fictional world slowly and smoothly.

> "Modern culture is fascinated with ever more transparent, lifelike media with the total immersion of all of our senses."[2]

---

[1] Ryan, 11.

[2] Ryan, 347.

With the added technology of *virtual reality*, one can only imagine the films of the future.

VIII. FILM MUSIC IS INTERACTIVE

"Meditation Investigates"

Not surprisingly, film music requires interactive listeners. It has an "interface" which becomes a probing exploration, an involved pursuit. It is the art of discovery. It is the main tool of serious make-believe. After all, the language of music combines the "expected" and the "unexpected." Without our active expectations, music would totally fail to communicate.

And it happens on different levels of intensity. Children, for example, live in imaginary realms with toys to represent the real world they're just beginning to explore. With films, we do the same, but on a different level. The best of today's music-drama is profoundly more than a toy.

For the novice, "interactivity" is more passive than active. It is timidly thoughtful, distantly reflective, and carefully contemplative. At best, the beginner allows his imagination to flow freely with meaningful possibilities. But this "passive-interactivity" may rise to no more than "mellowing out" in a sauna.

With film music buffs, though, this effortless wondering becomes a more active meditation. The twelfth century theologian, Richard of

Saint-Victor, puts it this way: "Contemplation wonders . . . (but) meditation investigates."[1]

These "investigators" purposely place themselves in a "real" unreal world. They confidently commit themselves to an unknown voyage, and they fully expect to cross boundaries. Their expectancy resembles the excitement of symphony conductors who hold yet-to-be-performed musical scores in their hands.

This level of film experience rises to an alert expectancy, watching for something to catch on fire. This is where journeymen begin seeing the familiar turning strange and the strange turning familiar.

They don't mind "getting caught" in this interface. They don't mind the disturbance of their assumptions and preconceptions. Indeed, they welcome the surprise, the serendipity, the fresh connections, the peripheral visions.

Often, we find this intensity among those who love viewing live drama and reading good books. They live the plot as their **own destiny**,

---

[1] Thomas Bestul, *Chaucer's Parson's Tale and the Late-Medieval Tradition of Religious Meditation,* http://www.jstor.org/pss/2854185

anticipating the unfolding of worlds—"I wonder. . . ." "He should. . . ." "What if. . . ." In other words, their raw reflecting becomes a spontaneous, real-time reenactment, receiving and sharing from the future that which is not yet.

Art is a Dialogue

Surely, we understand by now that film art is a "dialogue." It is a two-way process between the world of film and the interactive collaborator. It is a bidirectional, give-and-take, to-and-fro movement.

Between us and "it," there is a complementarity, a bond, a symbiotic relationship. Between our inspired imagination and the virtual image, there is a strange communion, an exotic discourse. Between two different things in close proximity, there is a continuous interaction, a total fluidity.

In short, this dialogue is a swirling, revolving reflection with multilayered meanings.

It begins when the film experience breaks into our world, when we are spontaneously compelled to respond, when we are suddenly impelled to create a newborn image or creatively understand one already created. At this moment, we feel empowered to act, to express something, to give form to our sensory images.

And, in our response, we "turn the tables": We break into the film's world.

We simply speak the language of juxtaposition. We boldly translate the original "object" into other media and other senses. We freely paraphrase the original images into unrelated art forms and unalike feelings. As in a game, we "put something into play." Or, like football quarterbacks, we throw the ball where the receiver is not!

We wonder, "How might this event be transformed if we boldly add our ideas to the original ideas? What may it become if we insolently add conflicting ideas to the original idea? What would it look like, sound like, feel like—even taste like or smell like—if we translated it into dance, drama, music, visual art, poetry, or . . . ?"

In other words, we explore the continuities and connections that remain hidden in the original sensory image. We interface the unalike. We compare things that cannot be compared, sometimes holding side-by-side other art forms and other senses.

Suddenly, our response seems to feed the first awareness, and we inexplicably receive an immediate "feedback." In other words, the world that music-drama points to grows in response to our probing explorations. We do something and it does something too.

FILM MUSIC

As a result, we receive a deeper understanding, a further significance, a richer revelation from the original object. So we respond again. And, as before, we explore differing perspectives of the whole. Over and over, deeper and deeper, we respond and receive a growing vision of an alternate world—multilayered meanings on top of multilayered meanings.

Again, it's open-ended.

This deepening is like being in a small town hidden on all sides by a mountain range. As we climb, seeking differing perspectives, each view increases the information regarding the town's dwellings and inhabitants. Amazingly, the town seems to change and grow with each new perspective.

IX. FILM MUSIC IS FELT MEANING

Pointing Beyond

We cannot define film music without defining "felt meaning." Everything we've described may be the "medium," but it is not the meaning. In profound art, hidden sensuous forces lie beyond ordinary knowledge or intelligence. As a result, great art points beyond itself. It passes outside itself. It speaks further than itself.

But its "medium is **not** the message."

In other words, it speaks indirectly. Meaning is realized through it, but not in it. All of its components—the intuitive, the nonliteral, the immersive, the interactive, and the tensions within the juxtapositions—conspire to represent something "not there."

Through insistent tensions between the realms of the real and the unreal, film music provides the necessary transport into a *third realm* of "felt meaning." With film music, the meaning exceeds its medium; its purpose surpasses its appearance.

It is "virtual." It is "vicarious."

The arts provide our examples: Henry Miller reports, "Art is only a means to life, to the life more abundant. It is not in itself the life more abundant."[1] Even a great masterpiece can't claim its own meaning, for "overwhelming beauty points beyond itself."[2] Popular movies may host multitudes of juxtapositions within and between drama, music, visual art, poetry, and choreography, but that's not what's important. Or, Ted Nelson puts it this way: "Who cares?"[3] What's important is the meaning to which these juxtapositions point.

Further, while reading a good novel, our main concern is not with the name of the author or his writing technique. We revel, instead, in felt meaning and the souvenirs of the journey.

So with film music, the medium is the signifier and the message the signified; the medium is the sender and the message the sent; the medium is the revealer and the message the

---

[1] Henry Miller, quoted in Brewster Ghiselin, *The Creative Process* (New York: Mentor Books, 1955) p. 181.

[2] Hans Urs von Balthasar, quoted in Patrick Sherry, *Spirit and Beauty: An Introduction to Theological Aesthetics* (Oxford: Clarendon Press, 1992) p. 161.

[3] Ted Nelson, quoted in *Vorticism*, http://tinyurl.com/3qounlv

revealed; the medium is the fantasy and the message is the certainty.

Admittedly, the "arts" of pop cultures and mercenary merchandisers often point only to themselves. Their worlds shout, "Look at us, look at us!" There's nothing wrong with a good showman, but little meaning emerges unless the performer and the product point beyond themselves.

A Leaping Spark

In music-drama, this need for meaning comes from our desire to understand where we've been and where we're going. Marie Ryan offers one example:

> Suspense increases as the range of possibilities decreases . . . The intensity of suspense is inversely proportional to the range of possibilities. At the beginning of a story, everything can happen, and the forking paths into the future are too numerous to contemplate. The future begins to take shape when a problem arises and confronts the hero with a limited number of possible lines of action. When a line is chosen, the spectrum of possible developments is reduced to the dichotomy of one branch leading to success and another ending in failure, a

polarization that marks the beginning of the climax in the action."[4]

So, sooner or later, we leave our reflections—our creative interactions—and cross a bridge to interpretation—the realm of felt meanings.

Until now, the story and the music have been in a fluid state—we might call it allusions on steroids! Then, suddenly we begin sensing unplanned and unexpected disclosures. Socrates described it as something "born suddenly in the soul, like a light . . . fired by a leaping spark."[5] Or, the popular writer, Norman Maclean, describes "seeing something noticeable which makes you see something you weren't noticing which makes you see something that isn't even visible."[6]

Those with more "experienced" intuition instantly discern or separate the shallow from the profound, the form from the content, the expediency from the epiphany, and the worthless from the worthy. And, just as

---

[4] Ryan, 142.

[5] Raoul Morley, *From Word to Silence, Vol. 1, The Rise and Fall of Logos* (Bonn: Hanstein, 1986), p. 95.

[6] Norman Maclean, *A River Runs Through It* (New York: Pocket Boo ks, 1992) p. 101.

instantly, they recognize or resonate with the harmonious insights, analogical jumps, and "surprised obviousness."

Boldly, we begin to "know." Something begins to tie things together, to take on form. This is an interpretive moment—a "defining" moment—where we give the object of our attention a focus. In other words, we remove the vagueness and doubt, and more clearly state its identity.

We "name" it.

A New Way of Knowing

Films are a source of wonder and wisdom in our time—a world of yet undiscovered, profound significance. For they are an advanced version of *profound* metaphor, and metaphor has already become central to all studies of meaning. Metaphor has become "central to aesthetics, the theory of literature, linguistics, and the philosophy of language." It is "discussed in psychology, the philosophy of mind, (and) the philosophy of science."[7] And it "will change the way philosophers answer fundamental questions.

---

[7] Daniel Gilman, "Book Reviews," *Modern Philology*, Vol. 89, Issu 73e 3, Feb. 1992, p. 462.

In fact, we now know that all human thought—including scientific thought—is metaphorical. All the things that make life mean what it means require metaphor.[8] So it comes as no surprise that film music turns out to be "a peripheral vision by which we perceive and articulate the hidden background of beings, the world or context in which they become real and meaningful."[9]

On the heels of the Enlightenment, where "knowing" results from a linear sequence of critical thinking with one final, "correct" answer, great films suggests a shift in "who we are within reality." Yet, they seek not to scorn or discard valid traditions, but to recreate them. In the words of Marie Ryan, we are entering "the blissful state of retrospective omniscience."[10]

The spectacular difference from previous "knowing" comes from the fact that film music is an "embodied knowing," where inspired

---

[8] George Lakoff and Mark Johnson, *Philosophy in the Flesh: The Embodied Mind and Its Challenge to Western Thought* (New York, NY: Basic Books, 1999) pp. 58, 59.

[9] Heim, xiii.

[10] Ryan, (above).

senses, feelings, and emotions become cognitive extensions of the mind.

Intervenes in Life

No wonder the experience becomes a personal event, a first person event. Often, it has "our name written all over it." Sometimes we sense, "This was just for me." And, in the best of times, they offer a permanent "becoming" or even an "irreversible . . . transformation."[11]

When Dostoevsky said, "Beauty will save the world,"[12] he meant that our sense of beauty will save the world. There's no impersonal, intellectual beauty here.

There is a role, though, for the rigorous, hard-won logic of the past that guards against selfish subjectivity, mindless conformity, and corrupt "niceness." But the beauty that transforms the human endeavor does not come from the "idea" of change. It comes from the powerful "felt meanings" of personal events.

The reasoned words of the modern era may "supervene" in life—that is, they may "add to" life. But the hidden "words" of film music can

---

[11] Pierre Lévy, quoted in Ryan, 35-37.

[12] Nancy Forest-Flier, "Beauty Will Save the World," http://bit.ly/ceJph9

"intervene" in life—that is, they can "change" life.

Priceless Souvenirs

When we first arrive at the interpretive—the felt meaning moment of our journey—we finish with the endless juxtapositions and their endless inferences. Stopping our interactions and starting our interpretations is good, for new insights remain short-lived without some kind of inventory. Now we return "home," perhaps even changed by the experience. At this point, we usually forget the "language" of the journey and remember now only the meaning.

Unless we share its significance with others, the journey has stopped, the revelation has stopped, and the empowering has stopped. Everything we learned quickly turns "preconceived." And, we soon realize what every farmer knows: "Leave the fruit on the vine too long, and it will spoil."

If we're honest, we eventually understand that we can't stay here. We're reminded that this journey is a never-ending, always-deepening cycle. For meaning must always take on new meaning, and we must always draw on the endless implications of an inexhaustible resource.

We may hold priceless souvenirs from our journey, but we must always begin again.

SUGGESTED JOURNEY

East of Eden is a 1955 film loosely based on the 1952 novel by John Steinbeck. It describes a willful young man who, while looking for his own identity, competes for the love of his deeply religious father against his preferred brother. Of course, this is a retelling of the biblical Cain and Abel story.

Of the three films in which James Dean—the cultural icon of teenage disillusionment with a tragically short life—played the male lead, this is the only one released during his life and the only one Dean viewed in its entirety. As a result, the juxtaposition of beauty and sorrow in the music below reflects both the film story and the story of James Dean himself.

The composer of the music to this film was Leonard Rosenman. He received two Academy Awards and two Emmy Awards. He also composed the soundtracks for at least 61 movies.

Before responding to the following questions, again recall our definition of Film Music:

"Film Music is the intuitive, nonliteral language of juxtaposition. Using the sense of sound, participation in this language is immersive and interactive, and the result of the experience is felt meaning."

Listen to the music and record your reflections.

FILM MUSIC

1. While listening to this music, what sounds do you notice most? Describe in your own words the general nature of the sounds you are hearing. Again, these are simply "first impressions."

2. What particular sounds would you remember a week from now?

3. Describe the sounds you like the most. Why?

4. Describe the sounds you like the least. Why?

5. If you were the composer, what musical instruments or voices would you add? What kinds of musical sounds would you join with the sounds already there?

6. If you were an avant-garde composer and wanted to add non-musical sounds to this music, what would they be?

7. While this music is playing, describe your own picture that would match the music.

8. Complete the details of that picture.

9. What emotions are involved in the picture?

10. Give the picture a title.

11. Have you seen an event similar to this?

12. Have you experienced similar emotions? Describe.

13. If there is a "message" in this music, how would you reply?

X. THE ROLE OF EMOTIONS, FEELINGS AND SENSES

"The exact means by which film music triggers emotional responses in its audience is unknown."[1]

Film Music and Virtual Reality

To understand how film music "triggers" emotional responses, we must first understand virtual reality. After all, the arts and virtual reality share the same definition:

> ". . . the intuitive, nonliteral language of juxtaposition . . . this language is immersive and interactive, and the result of the experience is felt meaning."

Today's "virtual reality" may have begun with special hardware—goggles and gloves, and a computer—but "our biological sense organs are no less signal-transmitters and -transformers than the goggles and bodysuit we wear for the immersive experience of virtual reality."[2] After

---

[1] Shipon

[2] Zhai, xiv.

all, great movies and great music are no less vivid to our senses than "flight simulators."

All virtual reality—including films and film music—is sentient. It moves within a rich and diversified sensory environment. It is the power within today's sensuous technologies and an almost complete habitat for mind and body. Still more incredible, it is "the first intellectual technology that permits the active use of the body in the search for knowledge."[3]

Everything about VR requires our emotions, feelings, and senses. The "information" in VR is, after all, "sensory information." It speaks the language of immediate experience and felt meanings. It is "present" to us simply because our actual and virtual bodies interact with it.

Ask the "gamers."

The Same Language

Since VR "speaks" *the language of juxtaposition,* we should not be surprised when the emotions and feelings of films speak the same language. Ordinary emotions, for example, occur one at a time—either you're happy or you're sad. When two or more emotions, however, simultaneously challenge

---

[3] Heim, vii, viii.

each other—set up juxtapositions between each other—it's a sign of something happening at a much deeper level.

In VR, sentient struggles—between joy and sorrow, the repulsive and the appealing, terrifying power and fascinating mystery—repel as well as attract. We find similar juxtapositions in the arts. African-Americans celebrate joy with the same music in which they grieved during slavery. Music always sets a mood, of course, but the most profound music sets opposing moods.

In the same way, sensory juxtapositions in VR cross to other senses. Called "synaesthetics," one sense can evoke another sense or one sensation can result in another sensation—as in "loud colors," "dark sounds," "sweet smells," "bright voices," or "velvet tones." Obviously, these are illogical, yet we live these tensions between one feeling and another. We not only "see," we also "feel" we are seeing.

These tensions can get even more complex: When VR takes us on a multisensory journey through simultaneous art forms—as in a movie with its drama, choreography, narrative, poetry, visual art, music, etc.—the multitude of sensory juxtapositions play the same role as Velcro . . .

. . . the more hooks, the better.

An Embodied Knowing

In VR and the other arts, "feeling" and "knowing" are combined. Of course, this notion is difficult to accept among traditional thinkers. They usually limit emotions to knee-jerk subjectivity and, sometimes, even restrict the mind to a body part located in the head. Any other "knowing" is simply not subject to scientific analysis or logical reasoning. Other observers think otherwise:

> We are supposed to be logical, rational thinkers but we're not. The mind is composed of a messy network of different areas, many related to emotion . . . Consciousness is a small part of what the brain does: much of what we "think" is really driven by emotions.[4]

And Fritjof Capra, the American physicist, systems theorist, and author, goes further: "*All* thoughts arise from and are shaped by the body."[5]

---

[4] Jonah Lehrer, quoted in *Book Notes* by David Mays, a review of Lehrer's book, *How We Decide* http://tinyurl.com/6x2uot3

[5] Fritjof Capra, *The Hidden Connections: Integrating the Biological, Cognitive, and Social Dimensions of Life into a Science of*

The knowing body presents two more problems for traditional thinkers. First, this kind of knowing is hidden, its insights are obscure, and it represents "a huge amount of invisible analysis."[6] And secondly, it is a spontaneous, instinctive, on-the-fly awareness that moves more quickly—and some say more accurately—than the reasoning mind.

Emotions and feelings play a crucial role in the decision-making process. We've always assumed that if we knew the right information, we would always make the right decisions, but "[A] brain that can't feel can't make up its mind."[7]

Of course, these felt meanings are not merely felt. Instead, they yield light with their heat, revelation with their warmth, and insight with their inspiration. That's why we've heard reports of a poignant memory, a visceral knowing, or an intuitive heart. And that's why we've previously known a palpable sense, a perceptive touch, or a profound feeling.

Sustainability (New York: Doubleday, 2002) p. 64, 65, 72. (my italics).

[6] Lehrer, (above).

[7] Lehrer, (above).

In other words, this knowing is embodied. This perceiving is incarnated. These searching prostheses are part of our senses. These cognitive extensions are found in our feelings. And all these fleshly faculties are "endowed with intentions and powers of decision."[8]

Or, put another way, our mind is "really just a powerful biological machine."[9]

We've always known that inspired feeling and intuitive knowing deeply require each other. Amy Lowell wrote, for example, "Whatever (this hidden knowing) is, emotion, apprehended or hidden, is a part of it." For "[O]nly emotion can rouse the subconscious into action."[10]

Indeed, film music has a large backyard to play in!

Emotion and History

Few realize we are in the midst of an amazing moment in the history of knowing. To begin, Western Civilization has always looked to the

---

[8] Derrick de Kerckhove, *The Skin of Culture* (Toronto: Somerville House Publishing, 1995) p. 150.

[9] Lehrer, (above).

[10] Amy Lowell, *Poetry and Poets: Essays* (Cheshire, CT: Biblo-Moser, 1971) p. 25.

---

ancient Greeks and Hebrews for its bedrock beliefs. But we've forgotten that these two cultures differed decidedly. The Hebrews, for example, embraced "felt meaning." The Greeks didn't.

The Greeks believed emotions were a sign of weakness and of little value to good thinking. Instead, they emphasized formal "ideas" of thinking, including the cold facts of formula, analysis, theory, and conjecture. In short, their rules of knowing formed a systematic philosophy.

As a result, Greek thinking was anti-mystery, anti-emotion, and anti-feeling.

The Hebrews, on the other hand, built their lives on far more than formal ideas. Theirs was an oral culture where the narrative of life was an aesthetic experience, and where nonliteral imagination, feeling, and power intimately required each other.

Their knowing often came suddenly from the rawness of life itself.

With the Hebrews, words emerged first from the body, from visceral feelings, ecstatic passions, and felt meanings. Though filled with enigma and paradox, these words became their source of strength.

Today, we would call the thinking of the ancient Hebrews "flaky," entirely too subjective. But they knew a secret. They discerned the difference between the emotions of survival biology (called the "flesh") and the emotions of aesthetic wisdom (called the "spirit").

So the Greeks and the Hebrews were different, and the race was on to see which culture would control Western Civilization.

The outcome of this contest became apparent when the Greeks took the felt meanings of a young and vulnerable Christianity and molded them into theological ideas. In other words, they brought classical rhetoric to the aid of a new religion.

Christians were grateful.

As a result, though, most would agree that today's institutional culture is more Greek than Judeo-Christian. Indeed, the soul of Western Civilization could be called a Greek soul. Our DNA of academic knowing, for example, is found in the formal, systematic, Greek *idea* of knowing. Through the centuries, history has taken occasional tangents into emotionalism, but today, respectable institutions strictly exclude emotion from critical thinking, and they often limit beauty to an intellectual beauty.

But the pendulum is swinging, and it's obvious that movies are leading the way.

A New Reality?

So virtual reality and the arts are breaking the crust of formal thinking. They are discovering meaning beyond the boundaries of literal language. And they are finding this power on the ruins of rationality. They are marking a shift from logic to felt meaning, from informed opinion to inspired intuition, and from the literate to the visionary. They are blending the scientific with the sensuous, technology with touch, and the Internet with intimacy.

> Past communication technologies have tended to filter out cues used in interpersonal communication, whereas, virtual reality allows one to add, emphasize, or enhance cues . . . to "share emotion" with others, to empathize . . . by altering the salience of facial cues, by creating associations.[11]

As a result, there's a new idea about what is real. "In the past authenticity had to do with proof. Today, authenticity has to do with feeling."[12] Realities are becoming real simply because our senses, feelings, and emotions can

---

[11] Cline, 123.

[12] Phil Cooke, quoted in *Book Notes* by David Mays, http://tinyurl.com/3tvqtau

interact with them. Increasingly, "Experience itself is what is real."[13]

In other words, the very structure of knowing is changing—not "what" we know, but "how" we know. "We are now much more open to the idea that thought is not always verbal, and that some types of thought are better served by expressive resources."[14] It would seem, "We are searching for a home for the mind and heart."[15]

As a result, we witness the end of a philosophy that simply thinks. Permissible knowledge and forbidden knowledge are jumping into bed together. Acceptable thinking and unacceptable thinking are becoming fast friends.

Felt Meaning or Knee-Jerk Emotions?

But how reliable are these feelings? We've all known emotions that have caused us trouble. We've all experienced the rampant vanities and self-indulgences of animal-like longings. It's obvious that many of our emotions simply smell bad.

Just like our centuries-old rules of logic, those who travel the realms of imagination will need

---

[13] Cline, 224

[14] Ryan, 60, 61

[15] Heim, 85

---

new ways to test the reality of our new "realities." We will need new ways to confirm the validities of our validities. In short, the mature leaders of this age will need "to agree upon conditions of verifiability."[16]

Few studies have surfaced on the difference between "felt meaning" and our more base—or knee-jerk—emotions. Trying to tell the difference between felt meaning and knee-jerk emotions is like trying to recognize your friends and avoid your enemies at a masquerade party. It's difficult, but we have to know!

Of course, we admit that natural emotions are a necessary part of life. Our ordinary emotions, feelings, and instincts are not bad in themselves. But they can become bad. Really bad!

Discerning the Difference

So we begin by asking, "What is the source of our feelings? What instigated them? What got them going? Is the source credible? Trustworthy? Is it worth the risk of responding with the interaction and immersion of virtual realities?"

Further, every emotion has its own "MO" (*modus operandi*)—just like in a detective story. Every feeling discloses its own nature, inherent

---

[16] Cline, 179

qualities, specific patterns, distinctive styles, and typical traits. These traits, by themselves, will often reveal what's attracting your attention.

Manipulators are often discovered there.

The best "MO," though, reveals "size." Does your emotional response to an event point to a small world or a big world? Are your reactions narrow or expansive, shallow or profound? Do your feelings look at themselves or beyond themselves? Are they locked into limitations or open to possibilities?

Knee-jerk emotions, for example, tie themselves to the environment. They blindly follow the temper of the moment. These moods are fleeting and fickle, blown this way and that way by any and every momentary gust in our sails. Often these are emotions for the sake of emotions, kicks for the sake of kicks. Of course, they nearly always spring from selfishness—self-interest, self-centeredness, self-preservation, self-pleasure, self-indulgence . . . .

To be expected, these moods come and go. They are temporal; they have no lasting value. As a result, they leave no meaning. They are meaningless.

Felt meaning, on the other hand, is larger than knee-jerk reactions. Felt meaning can paint a bigger picture. It can reveal a more encompassing fullness. It can soar with more certainty. That's the reason the language of juxtaposition is so important. Rather than simple, single, one-at-a-time, knee-jerk emotions, juxtaposition requires a multitude of complex—even opposing—feelings.

More important, profound juxtapositions point only out of the power to which they point. Again, when Dostoevsky said, "Beauty will save the world," he did not mean beauty itself. But beauty can often point to hidden, yet powerful, truths that can (and have!) saved the world.

If the source and the nature of feelings refuse to tell you what you need to know, then look at the fruit, the final results, the ultimate impact, the eventual outcome. Whether virtual or not, the emotions in a VR event are real-life emotions, and the final results of these emotions will always reveal the intention of the original event. In other words, the seed of an event finally produces its fruit:

Was the experience unhelpful or helpful, destructive or constructive? Are you now a victim or a victor; were you hurt or helped, overpowered or empowered?

Inspired Knowing

In summary, felt meaning in film music requires a new way of knowing. We will "know" through our feelings, and it will lead to aesthetic wisdom.

Alfred Adler said, "Life happens at the level of events not of words." It's no surprise we're learning to agree with him, for today we no longer find renewal in mere rhetoric. We no longer believe that meaning comes only from the chemical reactions in our brain.

This historical awakening comes just in time. With the increasing power of computers, the only power left for us may be the creative inspirations of juxtapositions and their resulting felt meanings. The felt meanings of the future will give hope to those "who wish to contemplate 'what is true, what is real, what is good, and what is beautiful'."[17]

This historical moment promises that life can be full of wonder and adventure, and that our emotions, feelings, and senses may provide far more accurate stories about reality. Of course, we will always need tough-minded logic to save ourselves from ourselves, but if we are to risk journeys into film and film music, we will need to be inspired by our emotions and take responsibility for them as well.

---

[17] Cline, 227

XI. THE JUXTAPOSITIONS OF MOODS

Our Story of Three Moods

In music, "mood" is the most easily recognized among all the juxtapositions. If we were to choose an alternate definition for music, as example, it could be: "Music is the dramatic conflict between opposing moods."

Three basic moods form the foundational story of human consciousness: 1. Struggle, 2. Hope, and 3. Celebration. The ancient Hebrews, for example, always remembered: 1. They were in bondage to Egypt, 2. They escaped, and 3. They celebrated God's deliverance. The early Christians had a similar story: 1. There was darkness in the world, 2. Jesus came to bring light, and 3. He triumphed over the darkness.

Ever since—in every century and every culture—worship services have included this general story: 1. Confession, 2. Assurance, and 3. Dedication.

My lifelong experience conducting the standard orchestral repertoire reveals the same. The music that forms the "living repertoire"—that body of works still performed today—carries the dramatic conflict between these three moods.

THE JUXTAPOSITIONS OF MOODS

There are many variations within each mood, but the resulting, simultaneous conflict remains. Here are a few examples of the many shades of moods found within the three categories. This reminds me of the 3 primary colors that, when combined, create every other color.

I. Struggle: anxiety, fear, panic, the Unknown, awkwardness, mystery, darkness, uneasiness, hostility, shock, urgency. . . .

II. Hope: assurance, trust, peace, love, enchantment, care, tranquility, tenderness, promise, harmony, faith. . . .

III. Celebration: excitement, exhilaration, euphoria, ecstasy, victory, utopia, triumph, achievement, success. . . .

Notice the first group is mostly negative, the second is mostly positive, and the third category is mostly celebrative. Great music forms from the dramatic conflict between group one and the other two groups. And, though less often, the most ecstatic or profound moments form from all three moods in the same moment. In all of these conflicts, the "winning" or dominant mood can quickly be replaced by one of the other two categories.

Of course, the most enduring and endearing works end with "Celebration."

Painful Beauty

The conflict in moods stems from juxtapositions of the "known" and the "unknown." The second group contains mostly "known" sounds—familiar, traditional, "close-to-home" fragments of melody, harmony, rhythm, etc. The first group, however, contains mostly "unknown" sounds—unfamiliar, disruptive, even alien fragments of the same musical elements. Beyond these major differences, minor changes in volume, tempo, and pitch can make subtle differences within each category (the differences in the "struggle" category between "fear" and "panic," for example).

How does music create such a universally accurate, multitude of responses within us? It's enough to say that it does.

As mentioned earlier, we have heard these conflicting moods in the Blues where the performer usually sings the same theme: "I hurt real bad, but it feels so good." Or, we have seen it at the circus where makeup and mime outwardly express the secret grief of the happy clown.

We see the importance of the juxtaposition of moods when music is restricted to just one mood. "Struggle," by itself, for example, eventually self-destructs. The musical audience can stand just so much demonic darkness and destroyed hope. Then, naïve, cheerful "hope"—alone—eventually turns shallow and empty. We find an abundance of this on elevators, at dairy farms, and in our malls. Finally, "celebration," without reasons to celebrate, reminds us of the bubbles in Lawrence Welk's "bubble machine." All of them empty.

On the other hand, consider the power and beauty of conflicting moods in the movie, *Avatar*:

Notice the dominant moods of struggle in "The Destruction of Hometree," "You Don't Dream in Cryo," and "Shutting Down Grace's Lab." Notice, as well, the encouraging moods of hope and assurance in "I See You" and "The Bioluminescence of the Night." Finally, soar with the triumphant moods of celebration in "Jacob's first flight" and "Climbing Up Iknimaya."

Perhaps, best of all, experience the rare, simultaneous combination of all three moods in the "Gathering All The Na'Vi Clans for Battle" and "War (Part 2)."

When my granddaughter, Sarah Joy, was young, she asked, "Granddad, Why is beautiful music so painful?"

Now we know.

SUGGESTED JOURNEY

Avatar (2009) is about an ex-Marine thrust into conflicts on an alien planet filled with exotic life forms. As an Avatar—a human mind in an alien body—he wavers between two worlds. The conflict involves a desperate fight for his own existence and that of the native people.

James Horner (1953 – 2015) composed the music. His music for the film Titanic, by the way, is still the best selling orchestral soundtrack.

In the following musical excerpts from the movie, write the main mood for each selection. Use the Roman numeral "I" for the mood of struggle, "II" for the mood of hope or assurance, and "III" for the mood of celebration. If the moods change within a selection, put a dash between them (example I – II – III). If two or more moods are combined at the same time, place them together (example: I/II or II/III/I) with the predominate mood listed first.

"The Destruction of Hometree":
http://tinyurl.com/ocdojv6

"I See You":
http://tinyurl.com/97lhzsy

"Climbing Up Iknimaya":
http://tinyurl.com/nr8wgrs

(Musical excerpts on the Internet are often removed and then appear in different places.

However, well-known excerpts, like the above, are usually found with a simple search.)

XII. "REALITY" OR "ILLUSION"?

As soon as we enter the world of film, we begin tearing down a wall that separates the real from the unreal. One reality begins to disappear and the other begins to appear. In the best of films and film music, the experience becomes . . .

> . . . indistinguishable from the real, at least in terms of perceptual and cognitive processing . . .[1]

Earlier in this book, we found the definitions of art and virtual reality to be the same. So we will now use our experience of virtual reality to claim a far more significant role for film and film music:

Another World?

Those who avoid make-believe worlds have complained, "VR has no reality . . . it's not really real . . . it has no proof of reality!" So between these cautious complainers and more chancy participants, we ask, "How do we know that we know?" What is virtual and what is veritable anymore?

---

[1] Cline, 154 (my parentheses).

We may "come to our senses" when leaving the theater, but for a while, we are immersed in an interactive crisis of "knowing." To begin, most admit that a film can certainly seem real, that the experience often feels real. After all, ***"Experience itself is what is real."***[2] Consider that our emotions, feelings, and senses are **bodily connected** to the virtual world of film art, and when that happens, the world takes on a **physical reality**.

Our immersion in this alternate reality is both sentient and serious. It is "an **event**, in the strongest sense of the term."[3] And its sensory data provides a lifelike experience no different from the real world. After all, both worlds are perceived through our senses. And both worlds are confirmed through first person encounters.

Indeed, the fictions of film often feel more powerful than the facts of reality. And consider the trends. The film industry will undoubtedly follow technology into the coming virtual world.

Already, Virtual Reality is so in your face that video games can literally scare us, make us feel nervous, or cause excitement. Our heart rate increases, our adrenaline level rises, and we may actually sweat. Consider the airplane pilot

---

[2] Cline, 224 (emphasis added).

[3] Ryan, 35-37.

who crashes his plane in a flight simulator. The emotional and physical affect is so strong it can change his life forever!

If that's not real enough, consider the money that changes hands in virtual environments. In some parts of the United States, for example, virtual real estate is more expensive than **real** real estate.

Then, there's the Internet. When immersed in cyberspace, we're aware of reaching the world faster, and we know this phenomenon in real time. Dynamic and spontaneous, this experience of time becomes a triumph over the limits of time. In cyberspace, we're also aware of reaching the world farther, and we know it as an environment that stretches into some kind of space. Permanently open and never-ending, this experience of space becomes, as well, a triumph over the limits of space.

These triumphs over time and space are not only imagined, but made real. Another world is simply there; most of us don't feel the need to even argue about it.

Furthermore, we could describe the World Wide Web as a global human brain in which the simultaneous firing of millions of "synapses" forms the collective conversation of a new coexistence and the creative collaborations of a new consensus.

How real do we have to get before we call it reality?

One thing is certain, we are seeing less and less difference between virtual and real experiences. Already, today's youth share a passion for something out there. Already, they are giving form to *vital* virtual realities, *veritable* realities, *hyper*-realities—realities *beyond* realities. And, already, they describe these experiences in *real-time* and *real-life*.

For the rest of us, we're fascinated, as well, with real-life media, and we want more of it. We're tired of mere passive observation; we want, instead, more active participation. We've had enough of getting kissed over the telephone. We want the real thing.

Beyond Both Subjectivity and Objectivity

Yet, are these feelings merely subjective? Are we shaping a selfish version of reality out of knee-jerk impulses, personal biases, and irrational errors? VR participants, after all, often begin with extreme skepticism and end with extreme gullibility.

Nevertheless, to be human—to have a personhood—to be a self—means we are set apart from the real, the physical, or the natural order of the world. It's the only way we can be knowers, perceivers, or creators.

However, subjectivity is not our problem here, because great art looks beyond ordinary knowledge and beyond the limits of a psychological world. It looks past both subjectivity **and** objectivity. In the same way, it looks past the distortions of its own culture and even the illusions of its own art.

Again, the ancient Greeks understood this. They called it *prosopon*, meaning "a face facing a face." The resulting tensions between these opposing faces pointed to a third reality or a radical otherness, which they called the *Geist*, *pneuma*, or spirit of truth.[4] (If this reminds you of juxtaposition, you've got the idea.)

This ancient/future wisdom comes at the right time, for today's youth demand transparency and abhor obvious artifice.

The Meaningfully Real

Whether or not film stories are only imagined, Mychilo Cline confirms, "Experience itself is what is real."[5] Sensory information lends believability to an event. But Philip Zhai adds another perspective: What matters in our lives

---

[4] John Panteleimon Manoussakis, *After God: Richard Kearney and the Religious Turn in Continental Philosophy, 3rd edition* (Bronx, NY: Fordham University Press, 2006) p. 145.

[5] Cline, 224.

is not just the experientially real but the **meaningfully real**.[6] Life, after all, is a network of meaningful events and significant relationships.

In other words, experience and meaning do not depend on the physically real. Consciousness differs essentially from the natural order of the world, just as our personal identity does not rely on the cause and effect of science.

> The world of touch, taste, smell, color, and music; of love and friendship; of hope and envy; of money and power . . . these things do not exist in the world of atoms, but within our minds.[7]

Further, "[A] vivid image is more persuasive than a sound argument, a captivating narrative more compelling than historical evidence."[8] Further, "beliefs, desires, goals, commitments,

---

[6] Zhai, 131, 132.

[7] Cline, 209, 210.

[8] James A. Herrick, *Scientific Mythologies: How Science and Science Fiction Forge New Religious Beliefs* (Downers Grove, IL: InterVarsitiy Press: 2008) p. 251.

friends, family, traditions, environments . . . are all relationships that cannot be ignored."[9]

Have we been wrong in our definition of reality?

An Inexhaustible Resource

Assuming that the experience of art may point to a meaning that is no longer imagined, but real, what kind of meaning could give so much credence? We'll attempt one version here:

Meaning is a powerful and unambiguous awareness that looks past both subjectivity and objectivity and requires, at the same time, the death of our limited outlook and usual illusions. In art, for example, we confront the "ultimately real."[10] What we see of the ultimately real is always a small but significant portion of a more comprehensive context, a more immense web of relationships, and a greater mosaic of patterns.

Meaning, within art, is the big contained in the small.[11]

---

[9] Ryan, 122.

[10] Louis Dupré, *Symbols of the Sacred* (Grand Rapids: Eerdmans, 2000) p. 71.

[11] Zhai, 2.

Within these multilayered meanings, we never seem to run out of revelation. There is always something left to be explored. Our journey gives a growing vision of the same thing, bringing differing perspectives of the all within the all.

"It is an inexhaustible resource."[12] Theoretically, we never come to the end of possible juxtapositions nor their interpretations.

This theory of meaning differs from past theories. Enlightened meaning has nearly always been the product of "words," not sensory experiences—the results of remote reporting, not personal events—the acceptance of external proof, not internal credibility. Even artificial intelligence gurus "hold that consciousness is no more than intelligence." But "consciousness is in fact not the same as intelligence."[13] When I need a close friend, I don't go to my computer.

Nevertheless, there is a role for intelligent or critical thinking and "the hard-won wisdom and timeless rules of the past." Yet, this logic plays a secondary role to the "experience" of meaning that we confront in the arts. It's after the shock of unmediated meaning and the new reality it

---

[12] Ryan, 35-37.

[13] Zhai, 121.

claims that our critical faculties verify and confirm the integrity of the event.

The "Real" Imagined?

It would help here if we were a little more honest about normal reality. I've suggested that the imagined may be real. Now, I suggest the "real" may be imagined!

> Physicists tell us that the universe is without color, taste, smell, sound, or tactile sensation ("Nothing is red or black, soft or hard, etc., except thinking makes it so"). For example, different frequencies of light (i.e., electromagnetic waves of different wavelengths) are represented within the brain as different colors. But, objects do not have color. Color does not exist in the "real world."[14]

Also, it's commonly known among scientists that what we call matter is actually empty space. And some matter—like dark matter—can't be detected at all, though it supposedly makes up 95% of the universe.

Or, consider string theory that divides reality not into four but rather eleven dimensions, ten of space and one of time. And remember that in Einstein's theory of special relativity, space and

---

[14] Cline, 209, 210.

time differ decidedly from how we experience them.

In all honesty, why can't we admit that normal reality is simply a set of illusions that we commonly agree upon? Why can't we also admit that both the real and imagined worlds are simply what we perceive them to be? If we can admit these things, consider how alarmingly close we are to a full acceptance of the realities within a film-story world.

"Phenomena to support that new (world) will obediently turn up," said C. S. Lewis, and "I do not at all mean that these new phenomena are illusory."[15]

An Autonomous Force

Yet now, we present the strangest argument, by far, for the realities within art. **Films are real because they are gateways to reality**. And that "reality" is real because it is **an autonomous force**. Consider this summary of Marie-Laure Ryan's comments:

> [A film] is an autonomous reality with a dynamic nature. It has an independently

---

[15] C. S. Lewis, Clyde Kilby, *A Mind Awake: An Anthology of C. S. Lewis* (Boston: Mariner Books, 2003) p. 237.

existing form of discourse that acts as a gateway to an unmediated presence. Further, it has the power to unfold into many worlds which are governed by the artistic necessity of their own rules.[16]

In earlier chapters, we defined film music and the several terms within that definition, including juxtaposition. Finally, however, we cannot define, master, or control the language that lies beyond the music. It turns out that film music is only a gateway to another even more covert language—the strange zone between medium and message.

In the beginning, music breaks the bounds of normal language, but in the end, something else breaks the bounds of music. In the beginning, we may creatively participate, but in the end, something else has its own way of being.

In other words, music's power is not in music itself. Like all great art, music points out of the power to which it points. Earlier, for example, we discussed how our creative participation in film music requires a dialogue. Now we ask, "With whom or what are we dialoging?"

---

[16] Ryan, 13-15, 44-47, 50, 54-57, 90-94, 177-186. (My brackets.)

And how can the other part of the dialogue be "autonomous"?

With film music, for example, something does something. It doesn't just lie there, lounging passively in our imagination. It doesn't just lurk in the dormant regions of our subconscious. It's active. It moves. Perhaps that's the reason Alfred Adler wrote, "Trust only movement. Life happens at the level of events not of words. Trust movement."[17]

It's the same with all inspired art. It is not of us nor by us. It is not the fruit of our heroic exploits nor the genius of our self-will. Great art manifests its own presence; it evolves by itself. That's why the film story and music do not submit totally to our control.

Novelists report, for example, that their characters live a life of their own. They are not easily yanked around. Harriet Beecher Stowe wrote, "I could not control the story; it wrote itself."[18] In other words, art encounters the tendencies and tensions of an otherness—a necessity that cannot be ignored. We confirm

---

[17] Alfred Adler, "Quotes by Alfred Adler" *Finest Quotes* http://tinyurl.com/3tbotwu

[18] Charles Edward Stowe, *The Life of Harriet Beecher Stowe* (Honolulu: University Press of the Pacific, 2004) p.79.

---

this when we watch a movie. We are not interested in what the producers, writers, or technicians think, we only want to know what the story is saying.

It's no surprise, then, that the message in movies comes with both compelling and opposing forces. It entices us, yet controls its own message. It draws us in, yet resists arbitrary interpretations. We may participate with our unique perspective, but the message seldom loses its intended purpose.

A film story, for example, can't be argued with or dismissed like an idea, and it's hard for the teller of the story to twist it totally out of shape.

As a result, the power in its message is confronted rather than invented. We are the discoverers rather than the creators. Often, artists say, "It didn't come from me . . . it came 'out of the clear blue sky' . . . and I was totally surprised."

The ultimate proof, however, of an autonomous power is its persuasive power. It triggers implosions within us and kick-starts every first day of the rest of our lives.

"That which glides across the face of the unknown takes on the qualities of the unknowable."[19]

In summary, there is something about film music that is more than imagined. What is it and what are the implications? Sanity demands answers, and the following response may not be enough:

> The "natural" and the "virtual" are either equally real if you anchor your notion of reality in the sensory, or equally illusory if you preserve the notion of reality . . . realities are internally real, no more and no less.[20]

A New Integrity?

Our traditional institutions do not have the tools to prove or disprove the realities of film art. So how do we bring integrity to this medium? What are the conditions of verifiability? Here are four paths that may lead to partial answers:

---

[19] William Irwin Thompson, *The Time Falling Bodies Take To Light: Mythology, Sexuality and the Origins of Culture* (New York: St. Martin's Griffin, 1996).

[20] Zhai, 33-35.

For hundreds of years, we have asked, "What's behind the perceived." Our many philosophies, for example, have inquired, "What is real?" and "What can we know?" The answers have remained frustratingly unanswered. Now, however, VR is "likely to lead to new ideas about the nature of reality."[21] So our first pathway may be the use of virtual reality as an ideal laboratory "for examining our very sense of reality, especially 'hidden' realities."[22]

Second, we need a new structure for reality because the one we're using needs to expand. Today, our nature of being is shifting. As a result, we need new sensory frameworks that bring coherence and stability to our experiences. This, in turn, will bring "an imaginative 'recentering' . . . of possibilities around a new *actual* world."[23]

With a new structure opened up for us, we can then consider a third pathway that highlights the parallel versions of reality: one internal and the other external. Today, we see a disconnect, even disrespect, between the mechanistic world of science and the interior world of feeling. Perhaps the nature of being discovered in VR

---

[21] Cline, 170.

[22] Heim, 82.

[23] Richard Gerrig, quoted in Ryan, 15, 21.

---

could be placed on equal status with the laws of nature? Perhaps, we could find a new alliance of both mind and matter, feeling and fact.

Finally, VR might bypass traditional science altogether and join with advanced physics in discovering a reality beyond reality. An augmented reality. A hyper-reality. By the end of this century, the new world of VR may prove more real than what we now call reality.

In all the above possibilities, VR may redeem the real. And movies may find a new power of purpose and new reason for being.

Of course, none of this will happen unless we first understand the world of film and how to participate with it. Within its juxtapositions, for example, we must discern the difference between dead metaphors and live metaphors—between simple metaphors and significant metaphors—between common metaphors and complex metaphors—between literary metaphors and prophetic metaphors—between metaphors of expediency and metaphors of epiphany . . . .

We will recognize these differences most distinctly when we access a source independent of film music itself—an autonomous source.

SUGGESTED JOURNEY

Lawrence of Arabia is about a colorful and even scandalous British military officer and his divided loyalties during World War I in the Middle East. The music to the film excels in creating a sense of person and place: a thoroughly British soldier caught in the mysteries of Arabia.

The sound track was composed by the French composer, Maurice Jarre (1924 – 2009). Though classically trained, he was best known for his film scores. He was nominated for nine Academy Awards, and won three awards in the Best Original Score category for *Lawrence of Arabia* (1962), *Doctor Zhivago* (1965), and *A Passage to India* (1984).

Before responding to the following questions, recall, again, our definition of Film Music:

"Film Music is the intuitive, nonliteral language of juxtaposition. Using the sense of sound, participation in this language is immersive and interactive, and the result of the experience is felt meaning."

Listen to the music and share your reflections: http://tinyurl.com/o8vkep7

1. While listening to this music, what sounds do you notice most? Describe in your own words the general nature of the sounds you are

hearing. As before, these are "first impressions."

2. What particular sounds would you remember a week from now?

3. Describe the sounds you like the most. Why?

4. Describe the sounds you like the least. Why?

5. If you were the composer, what musical instruments or voices would you add? What kinds of musical sounds would you join with the sounds already there?

6. If you were an avant-garde composer and wanted to add non-musical sounds to this music, what would they be?

7. While this music is playing, describe your own picture that would match the music.

8. Complete the details of that picture.

9. What emotions are involved in the picture?

10. Give the picture a title.

11. Have you seen an event similar to this?

12. Have you experienced similar emotions? Describe.

13. If there is a "message" in this music, how would you reply?

XIII. THE ETHICS OF ILLUSION

Hell or Paradise?

There's a warning in this wonderland.

To put it bluntly, film art provides a world where deception usually plays a greater role than discernment. After all, "a counterfeit reality indistinguishable from the real"[1] is one of the definitions of art. So with such consensual hallucination,[2] a film could reverse itself, "revealing unintended consequences."[3]

In other words, future movie industries could go either way. We have much to gain or much to lose. The future is filled with both "exciting possibilities and frightening visions."[4] Surely we can imagine that "[A] trip taken anywhere out

---

[1] Cline, 171, 172.

[2] Heim, 79, 80.

[3] Shane, 37, 38.

[4] Cline, 272.

of the world can lead to hell as likely as to paradise."[5]

Even before the modern world of movies, we never had our feet on the ground anyway. So giving the world the unlimited sensations of technology reminds me of giving a drunk a cup of coffee: All you get is a wide-awake drunk.

History reveals endless disturbing stories of people's actions falling prey to questionable subjectivities, trivialities, manipulations, and deceptions. Today's fads, cheap thrills, empty forms, and vacuous divergences are no different. What are different are our rewired brains! This is the first generation to grow up with digital technology in their homes from birth. For better or worse, this is the first generation to be hardwired for a 24/7 alternate reality.

Stopping this generation from an almost total migration into virtual worlds is like stopping a tsunami with sand bags.

Obviously, these kids are fascinated with "movies on the go." Like moths attracted to flames,[6] they are lured, entranced, and even obsessed by it, and their parents are just as gullible. They began as mere voyeurs, but have

---

[5] Ryan, 77, 80, 85.

[6] Heim, 85.

ended by abandoning themselves to all the amazing new electronic products. They've always dreamed of Utopia, and now they have online communities like *Second Life* where they enjoy "gambling without loss, love without heartbreak, sex without exposure, (and) experience without risk."[7]

Maybe all this would be acceptable if we better understood what's going on. There's a vast difference between films that saturate unthinking lives and films that emerge from conscious lifestyles. Yet, not only do we fail to understand how it all works, we don't even realize when we're trapped.

Anything Goes

We're vulnerable. Endless tricks can manipulate and fool us. Anything can become a misleading mirage—a malicious make-believe—or a beguiling fool's paradise. Technology infused film could simply magnify these illusions; it could simply empower these illusory facts. Just because something "seems" does not always make it real.

Further, this is the first technology in history where children and teens hold "box-office" power. It's "a land without supervision, without

---

[7] Guest (above).

---

boundaries or direction."[8] Obviously, today's youth are not programmed for such empowerment.

In general, civilization is not prepared for this journey either. For the problem worsens in the context of our postmodern society. In the postmodernist West, everything is subjective. There is no universal truth, tradition, sense, or significance. Meanings are mutable, multiple, fluid, and fluctuating.

The result is an anything goes, loosey-goosey world with unbridled license. We are "increasingly lost in a sea of different opinions and perspectives."[9] Our realities are increasingly repackaged with cut-and-paste values, in-your-face anarchies, and rigged worlds.

Mixing postmodernism and film art in the same pot results in a very unstable historical stew. Admittedly, postmodernism has discarded many of the old, worn-out arguments we've used to prop ourselves up with. But in the process, it has also dismissed valuable information and traditions.

---

[8] Hipps, 135-137.

[9] Cline, 49-52.

It's not surprising that we now have a postmodern hunger for wisdom. We are desperately looking for the real within reality. In fact, it's not enough to be real; it's got to be really real. I suspect that's what's behind extreme sports.

Obviously, we need to rediscover the guarantees, evidences, and proofs of credibility, integrity, and certainty. And we need to do this for sanity, if for no other reason!

The Audience of the Future

Who are the digital gurus of today who will become the film audiences of the future?

For good or bad, most are restless addicts. They are driven by

> a primitive impulse to respond to immediate opportunities and threats. Such stimulation provokes excitement—a dopamine squirt—that researchers say can be addictive. In its absence, people feel bored . . . (These researchers) compare the lure of digital stimulation less to that of drugs and alcohol than to food

and sex, which are essential but counterproductive in excess.[10]

We had hoped that the best of the digital world would enhance life rather than escape it. But many participants are simply "agitated surfers of trivial information . . . restlessly splashing about in the shallows."[11] Their daily lives center on "information transfer"—the more information, the less analysis, pondering, and resulting wisdom. This constant information binge reminds me of the game, Trivia, where a profusion of mental energy ends up in pure waste.

Of course, wild and reckless speed accompanies their surfing. Erratic and impulsive, time hurtles past without concern for its outcome. The prize becomes "kicks for the sake of kicks"—as long as the "kicks" are immediately gratified.

Obviously, some carry immersion too far. There's a difference between being immersed in another world and being lost in it. Some of the most recklessly-willing submit themselves—

---

[10] Matt Richtel, "Attached to Technology and Paying a Price" *New York Times,* June 6, 2010, http://tinyurl.com/38t2ot5 (my parentheses)

[11] Benjamin Wiker, "The St. Augustine Challenge" *ToTheSource* January http://tinyurl.com/3jrwa2y

body, spirit, and soul—to a machine. They lose focus. They become totally consumed. They "zombie out." Even train engineers, airplane pilots, and commercial drivers have become so mesmerized by their screens—while on the job—that they've caused massive accidents or near accidents.

Being lost or consumed means people are already neglecting the real world. They can no longer respond fully to normal moments. They exist virtually everywhere except in the physical world. And they are unable to find meaning in the offline life that surrounds them.

In other words, they are nomads, roaming about with no fixed home. Is that their plan?

> A new mythology of technology is suggesting that nature doesn't matter anymore. We even hear talk of the transhuman or posthuman era in which people are optimally enhanced by technology . . . (These descriptions) immediately conjure images of Blade Runner, Mad Max or Cormac McCarthy's The Road: a post-apocalyptic dystopia stripped of nature.[12]

------

[12] Richard Louv, author of *The Nature Principle,* in an interview on *ToTheSource* http://tinyurl.com/3wzcqy2

Must we remind ourselves of the restorative power of nature, family, and friends? Must we admit there is something profoundly human in connecting deeply with our environment and with each other?

Yet, even when they want to, it's almost impossible for most digital vagrants to make these basic connections.

Seraph and Snake

The disconnection from basic personal relationships poses a serious problem, for there's bad stuff out there. In a virtual world, seraph and snake live side by side. There are no rules, no safeguards. Everyone is for himself.

In other words, there is a dark side to a technology-based art,

> . . . including the online criminals who plague imaginary worlds, from cyber mafiosos and prostitutes to real hackers and terrorists. It seems that one cannot escape greed, corruption, and human weakness–even inside a computer screen.[13]

Frankly, the rest of us are less virtuous than we've imagined. Bullying, for example, remains common and out of control. Still more ominous,

---

[13] Guest, (above).

online behavior could easily influence offline behavior. "In the long run, one might expect to see the breakdown of real-world practices and institutions . . . If nation-states are unable to maintain boundaries, to regulate commerce, and to enforce laws, it is likely to result in social and economic upheaval."[14]

Some gurus design art with the relished intent to lie. Coupling enormous skill with dubious character, these deceptive and destructive gurus operate in the realm of artifice rather than art.

Alarmingly, as well, are questions of health. Some environments are seriously pathological. Many participants, for example, believe if an experience is crazy enough, senseless enough, they must be having fun. So they become intrigued with and drawn toward anything wild or otherworldly. Any weirdness can be a sure sign of adventure. These adventures, however, can have an eroding effect on a person's sense of self and can result in utterly deformed perspectives.

At some point these diseased realities can swell to uncontrollable proportions and there seems no escape from the monsters within. Then,

---

[14] Cline, 3, 226-228.

Marie Ryan states, "They enter your being, or rather you enter theirs."[15]

Role-playing—so typical in the digital world—is also one such manifestation that can contribute to a loss of identity. It "poses a question that goes to the very heart of fantasy, namely: What does the urge to become someone else tell us about ourselves?"[16]

Other than the above "possessed" participants, how many surfers simply burn out? "The age of the networked economy, of blurred time zones, puts enormous pressure on the individual . . . It becomes hard to shut off the day, recuperate, and relax when the day itself does not shut off." And, how many are "burned out on too many videos, too much porn, too many online games, too much conversation . . . and ultimately, just too many . . . experiences?"[17]

---

[15] Ryan 77, 80, 85.

[16] Ethan Gilsdorf, *Fantasy Freaks and Gaming Geeks: An Epic Quest for Reality Among Role Players, Online Gamers, and Other Dwellers of Imaginary Realms*, A review in the Product Description: http://tinyurl.com/3quumxf

[17] Tom Hayes, *Jump Point: How Network Culture is Revolutionizing Business* (Columbus, OH: McGraw-Hill, 2008) pp. 101, 183.

The Edge of a Precipice

Unbelievably, even darker threats loom in the future technologies of film.

> Each new power won by man is a power over man as well . . . Human nature will be the last part of Nature to surrender to Man . . . For once we treat human nature as mere clay, and take upon ourselves the role of master potter, there is no limit to what we can or will do.[18]

Already, for example, futurists plan using Virtual Reality for social engineering.[19] They intend to apply the powers of VR in shaping human behavior and punishing misconduct. As in Aldous Huxley's *Brave New World*, everyone will be turned into a happy slave through applied science. This form of social engineering will certainly be "more enslaving than liberating if controlled by a power-hunger state authority."[20]

Of course, film makers are not there yet, but why won't they be?

---

[18] C.S. Lewis in *The Abolition of Man* (New York: HarperCollins, 2001).

[19] Cline, 228.

[20] Zhai, 123, 124.

Several other concerns remain regarding the emerging possibilities of film technology and its role in our lives. As new technologies dangerously redefine what it means to be a human being, our foundational ethics risk similar dangers. After all, we may become what we behold.

> "(The future is) like a frightened horse that flies off into a gallop toward the edge of a precipice, wishing to stop, yet knowing that he cannot."[21]

Self-Defense

So, in an unethical world, what will we do? How will we protect ourselves? What will mental health look like in those circumstances?

To begin, we firmly root our core self before even leaving the physical world or the normal known world. That includes an inner discipline, strengthened will, informed belief system, and inclusion in a community. Most important, a strengthened self includes a structure which surrounds you with those you trust, those who love you, and those who feel responsible for you.

Obviously, we must also know and understand the powers of the virtual experience.

---

[21] Ryan, 77, 80, 85.

Then, **you decide** when and where to enter this alternative world. **You select** the frequency of your experiences and the duration of those experiences. **You choose** what enters your eyes and ears. In short, take the initiative to simply exercise the determined freedom of your own choice.

Artists, for example, would go mad without preset limits. A composer needs to know the instruments, the voices, the key, the length, the purpose, and so on, before beginning to compose. All artists—sooner or later—need to know the parameters within which they will work.

Finally, before launching your trip, it's best to feel rested and to ask a friend to hold you accountable for your decisions.

Self-Assessment

Of course, participants should already be living conscious lifestyles before a virtual journey. During the experience itself, it is important for participants to be especially aware, especially awake. This awareness is like seeing yourself see. It's like consciousness of consciousness. It's like being on the outside looking in. In other words, we stand to one side and reflect on something totally outside our self. Instead of feeling without seeing, we see as well as feel.

With this constant self-assessment, we can keep things in perspective as we continually remind ourselves of the medium we are in.

And we stay in control. A healthy dose of skepticism alive and active within our critical faculties is an especially important tool. We become conservative daredevils, cautious prophets. After all, our responses can be either voluntary or involuntary. We decide.

Yes, immersion is part of the experience, but we determine to be immersed without making it our home, getting lost, getting consumed, or sinking into the depths. Again, we can be safely immersed and still appreciate the journey.

This kind of immersion is like the actress who plays the role of an evil person knowing all along she has no empathy for the character she's playing. She simply remains on the outside looking in.

Or, this kind of immersion reminds me of the story of Coronado—the first European to explore the United States Southwest. He walked across the endless plains of waste-high buffalo grass where there were no trees or landmarks to prevent getting lost. Coronado's men were so terrified, they drove a stake in the ground ever so often to safely find their way back. That land is still called Llano Estacado—the "Staked Plains."

So, in summary, stay aware!   We become puppets otherwise.

Discerning Gatekeepers

But films are "proactive,"—they "act on us"—so our awareness should also be proactive—more so than we've suggested thus far. We actively look for signs of a hidden agenda. We actively discern differences between what helps and hurts. A virtual experience never appears out of nothing. It always comes with either discovery or destruction.

So we become gate keepers. We don't allow just anything and everything to enter our eye-gates or our ear-gates. And we certainly should not put up with gate-crashers. We actively seek and search out warning signs.

Some film moguls seek power and wealth at the participant's expense. So we look for cunning plans or devices intended to trick or deceive us. For example, they design self-reflective worlds their customers will think most credible, and we willingly pay for trips through their hall of mirrors. And a good director will "manipulate the hell out of an audience."[22]

Of course, negative and destructive experiences are easily discerned. And, there's nothing wrong

---

[22] *Francis Sonne, "Readings in Drama"* http://tinyurl.com/3rrt2zk

with the drama between "light" and "dark" forces. That story has been enacted since the beginning of stories. When the drama goes into a tail spin, however, and ends in total chaos—total destruction—questions should be raised about its usefulness or purpose for the individual participant.

Films marked by pessimism, fatalism, and menace already inhabit their own genre. *Film noir* was originally applied by French critics to American thriller and detective movies made in the decade after 1944. The term was also applied to film directors like Orson Welles, Fritz Lang, and Billy Wilder.

In addition to looking for designers' deceptions, we also look for our own errors. Often, though, we remain unaware and step into the very muck we seek to avoid. Driving my car with the radio tuned to what I consider "unredeemable" music, I sit there annoyed until I remind myself, "Wait a minute. This is not a concert. I have a choice (click)."

Of a more serious nature, however, we should constantly watch for a loss of identity and a loss of control. When we forget ourselves, forget who and where we are, we can sink into the depths. We must be especially careful with "role-playing"—living the fantasy of being another person.

Far too typically, though, we miss it when the story points only to itself. We like to say, "The medium is the message." But with a virtual experience, this is not true. In fact, we so often mistake the medium for the message that we confuse the oyster for the pearl. We consume, as example, the latest novelty, fad, style, taste or decor and think, "That's it . . . that was fun." (No message, just a fun medium.) Or, we admire the work of skillful writers with their colorful idioms, rhetorical flourishes, and clever figures of speech and think, "Brilliant . . . the critics will love this." (No message, just skillful rhetoric.)

It is essential to remember that the meaning of a profound virtual experience is realized **through** the experience, not **in** the experience. Its meaning exceeds its medium; its purpose surpasses its appearance. It moves outside itself, points beyond itself, speaks apart from itself. So in our discernment, we should avoid mistaking the medium for the message. We should turn away from an interesting experience that parades only itself.

Closely related to this is the discernment of emotions. Some feelings and senses are simply knee-jerk emotions—natural, animal-like, while some represent what we have called felt-meaning. As gatekeepers, then, we separate the shallow from the profound, the worthless from the worthy.

Returning Home

Finally, we avoid staying too long in this alternate reality. The drama of the story and its music should be treated as a temporary immersion. It is not intended to be an addiction. After all, the best protection from a virtual experience is to safely return home—to return to an absolute world.

To enable that return, we force a final juxtaposition: We name the event. Regardless of the film title, we provide our own title. We set aside all mystery, vagueness, and doubt and boldly state its identity. Once you name it, it no longer has power over you. In fact, you have power over it.

Upon departure, we come to our own conclusions about what the journey meant, what the final message said. And, once again, we discern what to take with us and what to leave behind. Is it helpful? Is it relevant? Will it bring new and helpful relationships to myself, others, and life itself?

Back home, we reconnect with our self, others, and the natural world. Perhaps, we spend some time alone, write in a diary, or enjoy a hobby. Perhaps, we phone our friends, visit those we love, or nurture relationships in the community. And, perhaps, we go walking, mow the lawn, or play tennis. It is important to keep the roots of our lives nurtured with attention.

The Historical Call

Discernment—the choice between right and wrong, helpful and unhelpful—has been the same throughout history. The very historicity of the human experience has been our beacon for centuries. In every age, we reaffirm those deep-rooted, abiding, enduring values and, within those values, we rediscover honesty, honor, integrity, credibility, and certainty.

The ancient Hebrew culture knew and lived virtual experiences—probably more than anyone today. Their culture, for example, expected their citizens to "test the spirit."[23] And, those Hebrew prophets who lived on the edge, knew just how far they could go. Their culture and tradition would not allow any loose guns.[24] And later Christian saints warned believers against seeking ecstasy for its own sake.

And Aristotle, in the ancient Greek culture, taught the ideal of *eudaimonia* or "human flourishing"—the ethics of a good life. This had nothing to do with indoctrination, getting rich, or our inherent selfishness. It focused, instead, on the deepest engagement of life, the greatest

---

[23] I John 4:1 *The New Testament.*

[24] Robert R. Wilson, "Prophecy: Biblical Prophecy," *The Encyclopedia of Religion*, 1987 ed., XII, 17, 19.

feelings of well-being, contributions to one's community, close relationships, and the pursuit of personal aspirations. More important, it focused on the responsibilities of society's institutions—like the film industry!—to protect and further these ideals.[25]

Such wisdom parallels the suggestions in this chapter.

Still, we need new tests for new forms of ancient problems. We need to reframe the same ancient ethics, yet be mindful that, ancient though they may be, these ancient ethics are still appropriate for this world. Specifically for the virtual experience, we need "ethics of design" . . .

> . . . ideally . . . to extend basic human rights into virtual space, to promote human freedom and well-being, and to promote social stability . . . (The virtual experience needs) some form of technologically mediated environment—in which people are free to pursue their individual interests, without fear of harm or . . . an invasion of privacy . . . exemplifying . . . human interrelatedness

---

[25] Karen McCally, "Seeking *eudaimonia*" *Rochester Review,* March-April, 2014, pp 32-37

and responsibility . . . and with a maturing sense of right and wrong.[26]

Some of the recently emerging ethical issues include the role of the state, virtual rape, virtual pedophilia, the relationship between ethical and legal dimensions, and the ethical implications within illusions of reality.[27] Yet, Virtual Reality is "the first intellectual technology that permits the active use of the body in the search for knowledge,"[28] so ethical statements will be challenging, if not impossible.

Who will determine these ethics and enforce the rule of law? Or, will this be a new "Wild West"? If so, who will hold the ropes on all these wild horses?

In other words, who can be trusted? Will it be the geeks, the sensitive techies, and the pervasive cybersouls who hold the world by the tail? Will it be cinema moguls who have

---

[26] Cline, 169, 262 & http://fluxxed.net/?p=939

[27] Charles Wankel (Editor), Shaun Malleck (Editor), *Emerging Ethical Issues of Life in Virtual Worlds* (PB) (Research in Management Education and Development) (Charlotte, NC: Information Age Publishing, 2009) [product description] http://tinyurl.com/4yfyq4b

[28] Heim, pp. vii, viii.

perfected the technical arts of illusion? Will it be technology itself? It seems not—on all counts. "Technology remains incapable of repairing its own flawed nature, let alone our flawed nature. After all, it's our conspiring natures that have spread the conflict, sickness, economic disparity, and isolation for which we seek technological remedies."[29]

Nevertheless, let's hope we will have the humility, courage, and strength to respond to this historical call.

The Ghosts of Technologies to Come

This call, however, is not the call of an idea. It's not a plea for abstract philosophy. Yes, the virtual experience "will change the way philosophers answer fundamental questions in ethics, epistemology, and metaphysics."[30] But this is a *real* issue; this is where the rubber hits the road. After all, modern philosophy has rarely solved real life questions.

We have a lot at stake. The virtual experience has an interface, and that interface requires our involvement, and that involvement determines our fate. If any philosophy is involved, a

[29] Kevin Kelly, *What Technology Wants*, reviewed in *Collide Magazine* http://tinyurl.com/3t7bumo

[30] Cline, 155.

rampant virtual society needs the wisdom of **applied** philosophy—immediate and real. For "fundamental assumptions about knowledge, ethics, and what it means to be human are being radically deconstructed and rebuilt."[31]

Throughout history, each new technology has created more problems than it has solved. The torpedo, the hot-air balloon, poison gas, land mines, missiles, and laser guns were all promised to bring peace.[32] Is Virtual Reality another false promise? Will it be . . .

> . . . an accident of virtual reality annihilation or cyberspace collapse . . . designed by our fallible fellow beings? . . . our own misconduct? . . . a bug in the software? Anyone can command a tremendous amount of energy for many purposes in a split of a second.[33]

The things we see today are only the ghosts of technologies to come, and today's film industry is only a glimpse of a new medium in its infancy.

---

[31] Hipps, Shane, Flickering Pixels: How Technology Shapes Your Faith (Grand Rapids, MI: Zondervan, 2009) Product review. http://tinyurl.com/cm8y45

[32] Kelly (above).

[33] Zhai, 155, 156 (my punctuation added).

The future may seem to hold impossible possibilities, but the hazard is real.

SUGGESTED JOURNEY

The *Adventures of Robin Hood* (1938) is an American swashbuckler film, with music by Erich Korngold. The story concerns a Saxon knight who, as the outlaw head of a rebel army, fights back against Prince John and the Norman lords who are oppressing the Saxon commoners.

Korngold (1897 – 1957) is considered one of the founders of film music. Korngold's 1938 Academy Award for his score to *The Adventures of Robin Hood* marked the first time an Oscar was awarded to the composer rather than the head of the studio music department.

In the following selection from the film score of *The Adventures of Robin Hood*, you can easily imagine the famous sword fights of Errol Flynn. Notice especially how the music clearly conveys when Flynn is losing and when he is winning. And finally, of course, you can hear the victory of good over evil.

This excerpt is called "The Battle - The Duel - The Victory." Describe in your own words how these musical sounds portray Flynn losing, winning, or somewhere in between. The music is found about 11 minutes into this link. http://tinyurl.com/phn32rw

XIV. STUNNED BEYOND DISBELIEF

Virtual Reality and Film

The world's future intersects with the future of virtual reality,[1] including film and film music! Already VR's ubiquitous presence represents one of the great achievements of our era. And, looking ahead, I'm sometimes reminded of the film title, *On a Clear Day You Can See Forever*.

Today, we see the immediate and unsuspected historical ramifications of VR. VR is taking on a life of its own and is already becoming the center of social, economic, and artistic activity. Indeed, it is building a new cultural order. In the meantime, our knowns and unknowns are crossing paths in strange and exciting new ways.

Some observers feel terribly out of place, though. They're dragged kicking and screaming into the future, for they cannot reconcile the mechanistic world of science and the interior world of feeling—critical thinking and raw revelation—studious analysis and serious make-

---

[1] Cline, 272.

believe—cognition and passion—reason and reflection—management and memory . . . .

It doesn't help their discomfort that more than two thousand years' worth of philosophical questions remain unanswered,[2] and with VR, their discomfort only increases. The fact remains, however, that people no longer live doctrinal philosophies—they live VR. They no longer find renewal in rhetoric—they find it in VR.

And VR is oftentimes a film.

A New Reality?

One thing is for certain: VR promises "to transform, to redeem, our awareness of reality."[3] Though not reality itself, virtual reality may become the most profound medium of reality. It offers, for example, a new laboratory or lens through which we can more easily understand reality and understand it at a more authentic and profound level.

For centuries, civilization has endured the same timeless questions: "What is real?" "Who am I

---

[2] Bob Zunjic, "What is Philosophy," an online course, http://tinyurl.com/9uvgtt

[3] Ryan, 65.

in relationship to what is real?" "What can I know?" At a time when VR is changing reality as we have known it, and changing our relationship to that reality as well, we can hope to know, perhaps for the first time, the answers to these questions.

So VR may become the most profound bridge between our realm and another realm—the most unfathomed medium between the world of the observer and something "not there"—and the most immediate messenger between paradox and truth. Again,

> . . . all existential truth is paradoxical . . . (and) the language of revelation . . . (is) absolute paradox.[4]

A New Art?

Of course, VR is that "language of revelation." But VR is also the "Holy Grail of the artistic quest."[5] In other words, VR is the only hope for the arts. Yet, art is also the only hope for VR. Art liberates the creative power of VR so that, in the end, the creative process becomes one of the most essential roles for VR.[6]

---

[4] Søren Kierkegaard, quoted in Dupré, p. 58.

[5] Michael Heim, quoted in Ryan, 65.

[6] Ryan, 35-37.

VR provides "unlimited possibilities of creative interface."[7] After all, VR creates new worlds! It becomes the reality it proclaims even as it proclaims it. It becomes the world it announces even as it announces it. And today it doesn't simply happen in history, it is history. It doesn't simply predict the future, it fathers the future.

VR may be the prophetic answer to history. Though we often forget, our heritage informs us that the God of Western Civilization is the great Creator, not the great imitator, or the great spectator. And—according to the ancient Hebrews—God is always doing something new. That means the actual universe is the universe that is coming into being. It is not so much a Creation as it is a Creating.

Within that same heritage, we are made in God's image. In other words, we were intended to be creators—collaborative creators of the future.

"VR liberates the creative power of the user."[8] It "enables us to become unprecedentedly creative."[9] In other words, we are called to be co-creators with VR; we are called to be inspired

---

[7] Zhai, 156.

[8] Ryan, 65.

[9] Zhai, 158.

collaborators. We, too, summon worlds, create the future, and live in a not-yet realm. And we do this through juxtaposition—the language of creativity. Juxtaposition provides the inspired, never-ending, feedback loop between us and not-us.

> How meaningful our life is will depend on
> . . . (whether) creativity and purpose are
> the source of the meaning.[10]

Further, inspired creativity may prove our only hope, our only advantage, in a future world run by computer intelligence. There's one thing a machine can't do. It cannot be inspired.

Unfortunately, the notion of inspired creativity is a nearly lost idea of modernity. We commonly accept that only the creative can be creative. We commonly accept that creative events happen only at certain times and certain places. VR, however, may be the fortunate historical event that will break these misconceptions.

After all, VR opens us to the future

Unthinkable Possibilities

Today's breakthroughs represent only small portions of something largely hidden. And, without doubt, the future could seriously disorient us—even terrify us! The long range

---

[10] Zhai, 127, 128.

---

implications of always-accelerating technology will certainly alter the course of our lives. Ray Kurzweil writes:

> By the end of this decade, we will have full-immersion visual-auditory environments, populated by realistic looking virtual humans. By the 2030s, virtual reality will be totally realistic and compelling and we will spend most of our time in virtual environments. By the 2040s, even people of biological origin are likely to have the vast majority of their thinking process taking place in nonbiological substrates. We will all become virtual humans.[11]

A new physical world is imagined, as well. "With sufficient computational power, we can build all known laws of nature, and/or laws created by us, into the software . . . (It's) not impossible in principle . . . (Programs could create) a sense of physicality, even though they follow a new set of laws."[12] In other words, VR could become a complete habitat for the mind and the body.

Already,

---

[11] Ray Kurzweil, quoted in Cline, 190.

[12] Zhai, 67- 69 (my parentheses).

. . . a team of Japanese engineers dared to imagine a computer so powerful that it could keep track of everything in the world at once — steaming rain forests in Bolivia, factories in Mexico belching smoke, the jet stream, the Gulf Stream, the works . . . When they turned it on, the engineers did something no mere mortal had ever done before: they created the Earth.[13]

Will VR "allow us to participate in a process of the ultimate re-creation of our entire civilization?"[14] By the end of the century, could this new environment, this new world, prove more real than reality itself?

And what about us? Already there is a psychological consequence from the VR experience. Perception could change drastically, and with it, even the sense of life and death.[15] What would it mean to download your total personality so that your great-great-grandchildren could have a conversation with "you" a century or more after your death? "What

---

[13] Lev Grossman, "Earth Simulator" *Time* http://tinyurl.com/3nofnzk

[14] Zhai, xvii (my question mark).

[15] Nicole Stenger, quoted in Zhai, 53.

---

would it mean to live eternally in a digital universe?"[16]

VR and the New Imperative

We have a lot to learn! We must participate skillfully and creatively in this new environment. We must merge our sensory awareness with understanding. We must test, discern, and ground our evidence. And we must assume our prophetic role in guiding VR into a positive, creative future.

These imperatives are more than merely adapting to change, rolling with the punches, or getting some retraining. VR is moving too fast and too powerfully. We must get there before history gets there.

Can we imagine a world made of virtual reality? We must!

Either way, we will be stunned beyond disbelief.

---

[16] Jim Blascovich, Jeremy Bailenson, *Infinite Reality: Avatars, Eternal Life, New Worlds, and the Dawn of the Virtual Revolution* (New York: HarperCollins Publishers, 2010) Product review: http://tinyurl.com/3h7rnhx

Anything Goes

Consider what is already happening and its certain influence on the film industry.

Today's youth lead today's events. They love breaking boundaries and overcoming constraints. They revel in an "anything goes" world. They show an innate affinity with altered futures, and they stir passions for something "out there." These fast-tracking futurists celebrate their triumph over the tyrannies of time and space and welcome reaching faster and farther to everyone and everything.

In short, their fluid and eclectic lives move easily in a dynamic and spontaneous universe.

As a result, they welcome the collective conversations of a new coexistence—the creative collaborations of a new consensus. As mentioned before, their world resembles a "global human brain" in which the simultaneous firing of millions of "synapses" creates new patterns of "emerging" thought. Their universe has become a World Wide Web in which organic self-organization creates endless connections.

More important for the film industry, they have become impatient with passive obeisance to screens. They want to participate. They want to be on the "doing" and "sharing" end of modern media. After all, their video games allow them to invent part of their virtual world, to become creative collaborators in "world building." Their games, in other words, are no longer just for entertainment. They have become opportunities for open-ended self-expression. Constant interaction, for example, leads to constant change in the storyline of a sensually simulated world.

Their world is an open-ended dialogue with open-ended possibilities.

Permeating All Thought

Whether young or old, though, virtual reality is less and less a game. The notion of an "interface" or an "interactive" environment has "cut across our whole cultural world." "We are becoming . . . a culture more concerned with interactivity."[17] Indeed, few realize how close we are to a totally interactive environment.

People now have the power to do more than just receive information; they can choose whether or not to evaluate, reshape, add value, and pass the information along to others in the network. This power shift from receiver to connector will be the driving force of the next economy.[18]

---

[17] Heim, 76

[18] Tom Hayes, *Jump Point: How Network Culture is Revolutionizing Business* (Columbus, OH: McGraw-Hill, 2008) pp 30-31.

Within this virtual world, our culture is showing a preference for real people in real life situations. Reality TV provides an example. This could push the film industry past "representation art"—art that only simulates life—toward art as life itself.

Participation and interaction in a real-life, virtual environment will seamlessly integrate with our lives, permeating all thought, and moving increasingly off-line and off-screen into user's lives, as we migrate rapidly toward alternate worlds. The arts will become less limited to special occasions or time-appointed moments and will show up increasingly in everything we do.

This will change film as we know it.

Life's Interface

None of this should surprise us. Life, after all, is already immersive and interactive. It has an obvious interface. In fact, "The sense of belonging to a world cannot be complete without the possibility of interacting with it."[19]

Further, art is not a monologue. Between us and "it," there is a complementarity, a bond, a symbiotic relationship. Between our inspired imagination and its inspired image, there is a strange communion, an exotic discourse.

---

[19] Ryan, 67

Between our intuitive attentiveness and its hidden juxtapositions, there is a continuous interaction, a total fluidity.

In short, art is a dialogue with swirling, revolving reflections and multilayered meanings. It is a two-way process between the interactive collaborator and the realm of otherness. It is a bidirectional, give-and-take, to-and-fro movement.

In fact—when we are consciously aware—art shows up *incognito* in life itself—anywhere, anytime, and in any form. Moments not considered works of art become, themselves, works of art—often hidden, but there nevertheless. Everything points. Everything speaks.

In other words, art—and our response to it—do not limit themselves to special occasions, time-appointed moments, or the talented. Nothing is trivial. Nothing is insignificant. And nobody is empty-handed.

Finally, remember that our mind remains "a creative and enchanted" place "where most of the brain's work gets done."[20] Further, the

---

[20] David Brooks, *The Social Animal: The Hidden Sources of Love, Character, and Achievement* (New York: Random House, 2011) Product Review, http://url.ie/aupv

musing mind represents an "intuitive leap over the traditional step-by-step logical chain . . . it operates on a plane more sensitive and more complex than that of consciously controlled thought."

Seismic Events

Suddenly, the world is a different place, and the film industry knows it. Even "the 1990's and 2000's saw the collapse of nearly every single media tradition."[21]

But unexpected opportunities are arriving rapidly. With digital age breakthroughs, film moguls can now sell directly to their audience. The middle-man has been eliminated. This is a seismic event in the history of art, for it allows a new collaboration between the creators of film and their audience.

Of course, this joyful opportunity comes with the anxiety of "what do we do now?" These sweeping changes "will have far reaching implications for modern filmmakers, and will most likely destroy the traditional paradigms of

---

[21] Elliot Grove, *3 Ways Future Filmmaking Will Implode*   http://www.raindance.org/my-filmmaker-manefesto/

the movie industry."[22]

Nevertheless, filmmakers are already experimenting with "transvergence" or "second screens" which engage audiences across multiple screens and multiple platforms (tablets, smartphones, apps, websites, and television) along with the traditional off-line cinema. These interactive viewing experiences provide new means of storytelling, branding, and fan participation.

And there's more. At a recent "TransVergence Summit" for filmmakers, the headlines included "transmedia, immersive media, publishing, branded content, live experience, and multiscreen."[23]

Truly, something is happening.

First Person Collaborators

Regardless of present or future happenings, the goal will be participation—"first person" events. And that's possible only with "open-ended" experiences.

---

[22] Grove

[23] TransVergence Summit; Hollywood, CA; August 7 & 8, 2013
http://industryhappenings.com/event/hollywood-ca-transvergence-summit/

Yet, what is "open-ended"?

Irrespective of genre, great film art is about meaning and the creative power of the imagination. Rather than rules, it breaks rules. In place of limits, it transgresses limits. Leaping outside itself, it escapes a closed system. And, pointing beyond itself, it becomes open-ended.

Only then, can we claim the possibility of a creative dialogue with its aesthetic beauty.

Much of today's virtual reality—in all its forms—remains a "closed system." It's stuck in a limited, "preplanned" world. Take video games, as example. Designers create video games by defining them. The players must then follow the game's preset rules, and—if they win—it's because the game "allows" them to win. The players may show impressive skills, but the rules of the game are law. They may feel "creative," but in the end, the game only points to itself.

Neither great art nor our participation in it is a game we win or lose.

Or, take the example of "hypertext novels." We select—more or less blindly—the direction we want the story to go. But, again, we face the same problem. We can't creatively commit ourselves to any of the branching texts because all of them have been determined.[24]

Finally, consider the hundreds of movies with pitifully short "shelf-lives." Usually, they point only to themselves—commercial ads for a career, a name, or quick cash. But, occasionally, there comes a well-told story that points beyond itself, *out of the power to which it points*. The dialogue, then, is not with the story, but with what the story points to. And in that dialogue, we become "co-creators" of the experience. We become "actors" more than voyeurs. We give form to the depth more than merely standing awed by the depth.

We collaborate!

Serious Make-Believe

Someday, this collaboration will become a truly bold undertaking, a serious make-believe, a daring utterance. As we mentioned earlier, it will become the reality we proclaim even as we proclaim it. It will become the world we announce even as we announce it. For film art is not a "creation." It is a "creating." It doesn't

---

[24] Marie-Laure Ryan, *Narrative as Virtual Reality: Immersion and Interactivity in Literature and Electronic Media* (Baltimore, MD: The Johns Hopkins University Press, 2003) p. 20.

simply happen "in" history, it "is" history. It doesn't simply "predict" the future, it fathers the future.

Future film participants will speak spontaneously of nonexistent things as if they already existed. They will portray absent things as if they were present. They will dwell in a fertile, not-yet realm. In the words of Shakespeare, they will body forth "the forms of things unknown."[25]

The Canadian media scholar Pierre Lévy claims virtual reality "is the process of becoming, through which the world plays out its destiny . . . doing what mankind has always done, only more powerfully, consciously. . . ."[26]

Future films will enhance the power of art to transform reality. For, increasingly, we are "projecting a world."

Are you ready?

---

[25] *Cambridge Collections Online*, "Shakespeare Survey: Interpretation" Volume 4 http://tinyurl.com/4xfrhcj

[26] Ryan (above).

SUGGESTED JOURNEY

The Magnificent Seven is a 1960 American western film about seven American gunmen hired to protect a small village in Mexico from pillaging native bandits. The film's score was composed by Elmer Bernstein. In 2013, the film was placed in the United States National Film Registry by the Library of Congress as being "culturally, historically, or aesthetically significant."

Before responding to the following questions, recall, once more, our definition of Film Music:

"Film Music is the intuitive, nonliteral language of juxtaposition. Using the sense of sound, participation in this language is immersive and interactive, and the result of the experience is felt meaning."

Listen to the music here:
http://tinyurl.com/l5ph93u

When you are ready, answer the questions below.

1. While listening to this music, what sounds do you notice most? Describe in your own words the general nature of the sounds you are hearing. Again, these are "first impressions."

2. What particular sounds would you remember a week from now?

3. Describe the sounds you like the most. Why?

4. Describe the sounds you like the least. Why?

5. If you were the composer, what musical instruments or voices would you add? What kinds of musical sounds would you join with the sounds already there?

6. If you were an avant-garde composer and wanted to add non-musical sounds to this music, what would they be?

7. While this music is playing, describe your own picture that would match the music.

8. Complete the details of that picture.

9. What emotions are involved in the picture?

10. Give the picture a title.

11. Have you seen an event similar to this?

12. Have you experienced similar emotions? Describe.

13. If there is a "message" in this music, how would you reply?

Dr. Thomas Hohstadt is an international symphony conductor, author, lecturer, recording artist, composer, and soloist.

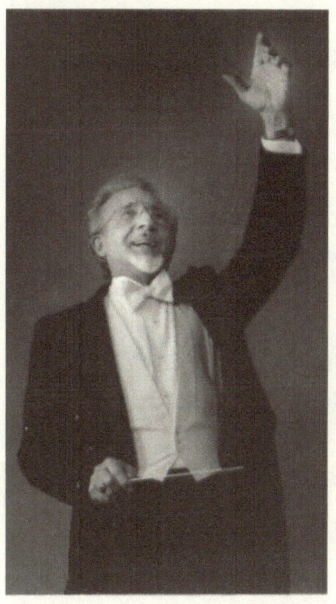

A Fulbright scholar, he earned four advanced degrees from the Eastman School of Music and the Vienna *Akademie für Musik*. In addition, he received the Performer's Certificate from the Eastman School of Music and advanced study from the renowned maestro, Pierre Monteux, at the Domaine School of Conductors.

A twenty-eight-year conducting career includes positions with the Eastman School of Music; the Honolulu, Amarillo, and Midland-Odessa Symphonies; and guest appearances in eight nations.

Hohstadt has long held an interest in film music. He recorded the sound tracks for Bruce Broughton's Silverado and several film scores by the famous Hollywood composer, Dimitri Tiomkin. And his recording of "Adventures in Hollywood" under the Citadel label has been widely received.

He is a contributor to *Cue Sheet*, the Film Music Society's Quarterly Journal. And his research into the Ancient Hebrew word, *damah*, became the basis for naming the Damah Film Festival. In this book on film music, he is the first to see the close relationship between the art of virtual reality and the future of film and film music.

A pioneer in the field of virtual reality, Hohstadt has shifted the focus from VR as a technology to VR as a language and art form. He was the first to add virtual reality to the curriculum of The University of Texas of the Permian Basin. He received the "Award of Merit" from *The Society for New Communications Research* for his co-authorship of *Voices of the Virtual World*. Recently, he co-authored "The Age of Virtual Reality" for *The American Communication Journal.*

Hohstadt has also been recognized for his achievements in the humanities. He participated in the founding of the Texas Committee for the Humanities, directed their seminars, and consulted and reviewed grant proposals for the National Endowment for the Humanities.

Presently, he is a Senior Lecturer at UTPB.

For more information about Dr. Hohstadt, visit http://tinyurl.com/lrrt9r2

www.ingramcontent.com/pod-product-compliance
Lightning Source LLC
Chambersburg PA
CBHW031048180526
45163CB00002BA/742